SWILL 2014

Neil Williams

Vile Fen Press

a division of Klatha Entertainment an Uldune Media company

SWILL 2014
Copyright © 2024 Neil Williams

Library and Archives Canada Cataloguing in Publication

Williams, Neil, 1958-
(Jamieson-Williams, Neil, 1958-)

  SWILL 2014/ Neil Williams.

ISBN 978-1-894602-33-4
  1. Science fiction--History and criticism.

2. Science fiction fans. I. Title.

PN3433.5.J36 2012   809.3'8762   C2012-901693-4

Published by Vile Fen Press
an imprint of Uldune Media
504 – 635 Canterbury Street,
Woodstock, ON, Canada, L4S 8X9.
www.uldunemedia.ca

Table of Contents

Introducing SWILL 2014

With 2014, SWILL moved to having unique covers for each issue.

The 2014 SWILLs completed the series on "The Taboos of Science Fiction" in the column Flogging A Dead Trekie.

With hope, you enjoy SWILL 2014

Neil Williams
August 2024

TRIGGER WARNING

SWILL is written to BE OFFENSIVE. Really, this is one of the premeditated intents of SWILL. It was written to offend back forty years ago and also just twelve years back in time.

It was not written for the sensibilities of those people under 30 years of age in the mid 2020s.

If you are the type of person who becomes so very much traumatised, that you have to curl up into a ball in bed for a week, after watching an episode of Friends where Chandler Bing talks about his father. If you thus find the 1990s sitcom Friends too racist, sexist, homophobic, and transphobic to watch, and you believe in the core of your heart, that this television series should never, ever, be permitted to air again and that all of the recordings and mastertapes of the series MUST be destroyed so there is now no danger that you will ever encounter this television show ever in the future; then SWILL is definitely not for you.

SWILL is offensive to many. That is one of the main purposes of SWILL. Read at your own risk.

You have been warned.

SWILL

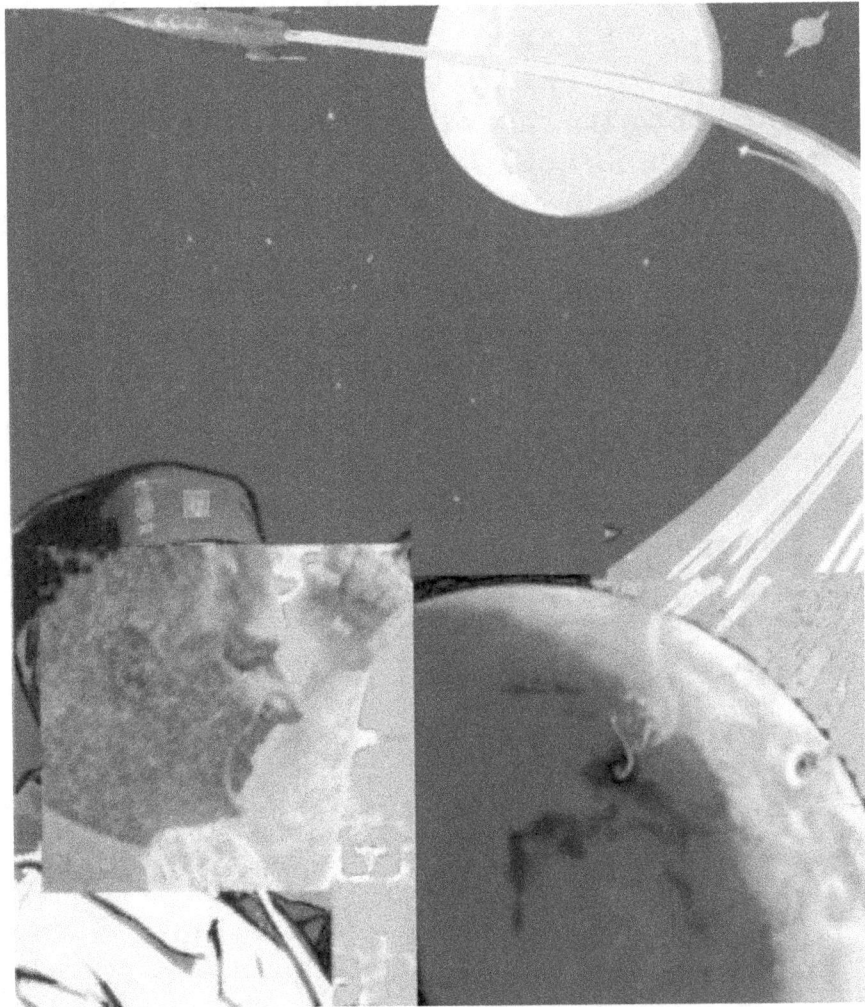

#23   Spring 2014

Table of Contents

SWILL is published quarterly (Spring, Summer, Autumn, and Winter) along with an annual every February - in other words, five times per year.

SWILL

Issue #23 Spring 2014

Copyright © 1981 - 2014 VileFen Press

a division of Klatha Entertainment an Uldune Media company

swill.uldunemedia.ca

Editorial: May Day Balagan

Neil Williams

It's May Day (or at least it will have been when this issue goes
live). And this issue is a May Day themed issue. Now, when I
first informed Lester of this (with a front cover preview) his
response was, "Truly alarming. Lester will beware of ice picks."
I informed him that the issue would not toe any Bolshevik,
Stalinist, etc. party lines and that he should not worry
regarding his (possibly) Trotskyite leanings and that he was free
to spout any false consciousness, counter-revolutionary,
politically incorrect (in the original sense of the term) drivel
that he so chose to do. He could even be reactionary and pretend
that the May Day theme did not exist. There would be no
penalties, assassination attempts, or one-way trips to a gulag.

So, why a May Day themed issue? Why not? It is the true
international day of labour, after all. And while, our masters
and their fellow travellers have been gleefully chortling their
victory over "communism" for the past 20 plus years; all is not
right in the world. Since the fall of the Soviet Union, the
Western democracies have been eroding democracy, in the USA, it
is getting harder to even pretend that they are not living under
a plutocracy masquerading as a democracy. Here in Canada, it is
a little better, but the current government has centralised
power, and with the recent Fair Elections Act (read - unfair
elections act) is further withering away our democratic system in
this country (the governing Conservatives are now back-peddling
on this legislation - we can only wait and see, and hope). The
growth of the Right-To-Work movement within the Western
democracies is also unsettling; where this ideology has been
transformed into legislation, the result has been the right to
work for less, reduced minimum wages, decreased health and safety
in the workplace, and laws that prohibit union membership. At
the same time, for the majority of the population within the
Western democracies, the actual standard of living has
stagnated[1]; taxes may be down, but user fees have gone up, and

---

[1] While there is the recent study out that states that the Canadian middle
class is doing okay, what the study really says is that the Canadian middle
class is just not doing as badly as the middle class in other Western

wages are barely keeping pace with inflation (if you are lucky)
or dropping behind the rate of inflation. Add to that the fact
that industrial capitalism is not very healthy, remember the
recent Great Recession, and our entire global economic system is
heading towards a wall at high speed; increased overproduction
and overconsumption will not save it, it only accelerates our
velocity and the wall is still there. FYI:that wall is the fact
that we live on a finite planet with finite resources - something
that is ignored by most economic theories or classified as an
externality (therefore external to economic formulae and
therefore unimportant) because most of our economic theories
claim, as a "scientific fact" that it is possible to have
infinite growth within a finite and closed system.

So, maybe the Western democracies were not as "victorious" as
they have claimed to have been. True, it has been a victory for
the top 10% and the corporate oligarchies. But has it been a
victory for the average person; I say that it has not been. I
say that we should re-examine the so-called left.

Before, I continue, I just want to place this on record (to
reduce the fear that the previous sentence - as well as the theme
of this issue - would induce for American readers): I have not,
nor have I ever been, a member of a communist party.

I have however, in the past, hung out with, had as friends,
dated, fucked, and lived-with card-carrying members of communist
parties. In years gone by I have dated and slept with women who
were members of the Communist Party of Canada (then Moscow line),
the Communist Party of Canada: Marxist-Leninist (then Albanian
line, the Workers Communist Party of Canada (an odd blend of
Maoism and feminism in Ontario and Maoism and soft separatism in
Quebec), and the Canadian Party of Labour (neo-Stalinist). In
spite of the best attempts by these women, I never did join a
communist party. As a sidebar: as it turns out I have never
dated or slept with a Trotskyite as I was always deemed too
politically incorrect by this variant (perhaps that should go on
my bucket list). And, to place further fear into Americans as to
my ideological contamination, most of my former commie

---

democracies. Not declining as badly as, say the USA middle class, does not
mean that the Canadian middle class is doing well.

girlfriends were members of the (Moscow line) Communist Party of Canada.

Why was I spending time with radical leftists; I was a radical leftist myself, just not a communist. As my former partners have told me, I am a petty bourgeois idealist individualist, with no appreciation of the vanguard of the proletariat or the discipline of the Party (and for the women involved in the CPC:M-L and the Workers Communist Party, I was also a crypto-class traitor). In other words, I am an anarchist - more specifically, an anarcho-syndicalist (not because I believe that unions will set us free, but because bottom-up workplace organisations are probably the best foundation - initially - for the re-organisation of society after the social revolution becomes a political one). I also at times describe myself as a libertarian-socialist - as this more clearly states where I sit for some people.

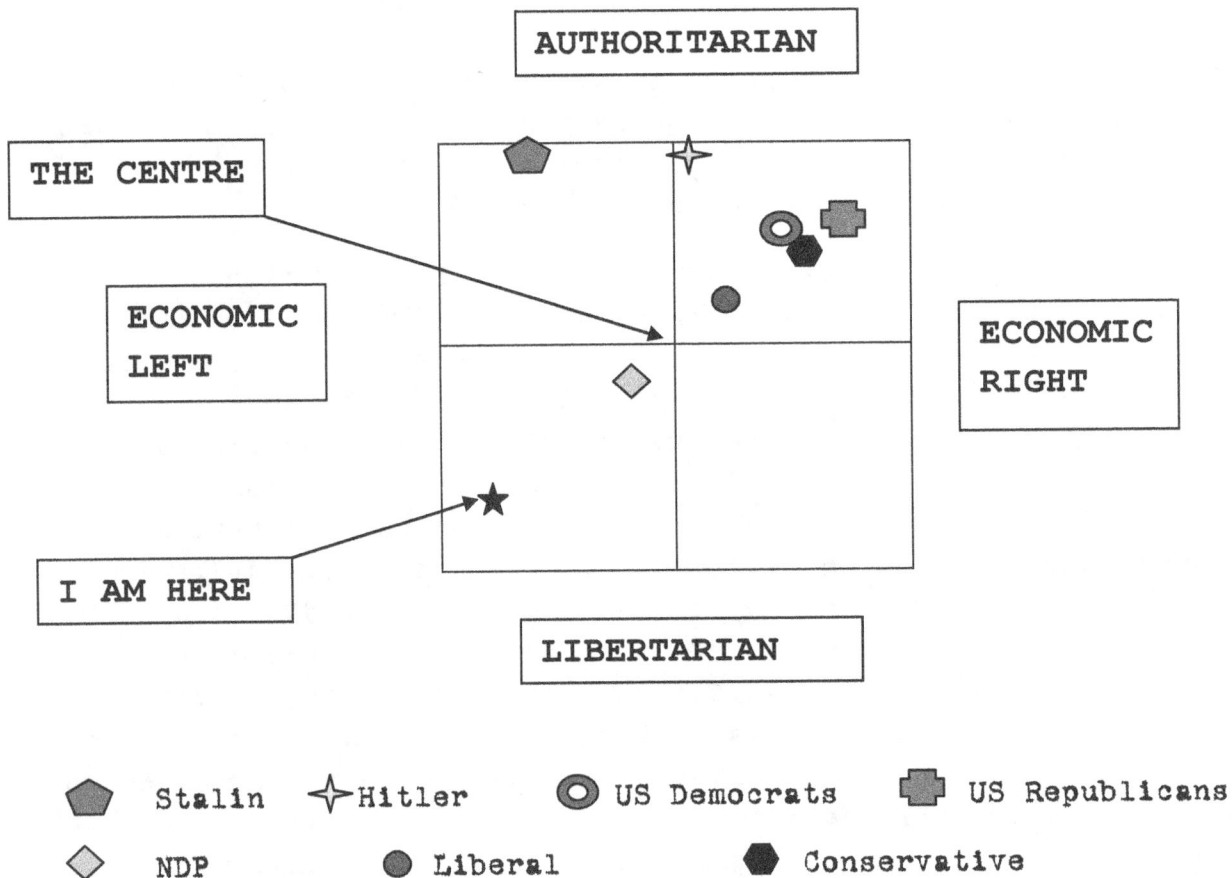

AUTHORITARIAN

THE CENTRE

ECONOMIC
LEFT

ECONOMIC
RIGHT

I AM HERE

LIBERTARIAN

⬟ Stalin ✦ Hitler ◎ US Democrats ✚ US Republicans

◇ NDP ● Liberal ⬡ Conservative

4

The above chart goes by several names, some of them branded, but it adds an extra axis to the old Left/Right axis. Remember, how they used to say that the far Right and the far Left are one and the same - far Right being fascism and far Left being communism. The addition of the Authoritarian/Libertarian axis[2], illustrates why that appeared so. For example, both Hitler and Stalin were strong Authoritarians, of the type we call totalitarians; Stalin was well over to the Economic Left, but Hitler wasn't of the far Economic Right, he was more a centrist on economic policies.

Regardless as claims made by the Conservative Party of Canada, the political centre remains where it always has been; this party is no longer anywhere close to the political centre. In the case of the Liberal Party of Canada, it used to sit at the political centre, or in a tight orbit around the political centre, but it has moved to the right to occupy the position once held by the old Progressive Conservative Party. The NDP used to be a little further to the left and has drifted closer to the centre over the past two decades.

The USA Democratic and Republican parties are shown here to illustrate why there is the Canadian joke about these two parties: "What's the difference between a USA Democrat and a USA Republican?" "A USA Democrat is sort of like the left wing of the Conservative Party and a USA Republican is sort of like the right wing of the Conservative Party."

Me there with my little black star in the lower left (Libertarian Left) quadrant am in favour of collective ownership of property (we are not talking about having to share your toothbrush or underwear communally, people) and limited interference by the State (preferably no State, though there may still have to be a quasi-State bottom-up organisation). That has always put me in conflict with most other varieties of socialism (including the

---

[2] Authoritarian: you believe that the government should be able to interfere in or tell people how to live their lives, up to, in the extreme, where the State governs all aspects of the individual's life, the totality of the citizen's life, or totalitarianism. Libertarian: you believe that the government should have little interference in the individual's life, up to, in the extreme, zero influence or anarchism (which means without rulers or without government).

ones that call themselves communism) as these types of socialism tend toward being more authoritarian. While, I do not support their means, or their ends (usually totalitarian); I do support their views regarding property and collective economic security as being beneficial for society as a whole.

So, according to neo-liberal wisdom, socialism is a failed system and should not even be considered for the future. Really? It is true that the state socialist (what anarchists call the forms of government that called themselves "communist" and which the Trots call "degenerate workers states" or "state capitalism") systems of the Soviet Union and its client states did fail. But what about the democratic socialism; did that fail? No, it didn't.

In Europe, where they are not the current government, where they are not part of a current coalition government, they are the major party or parties in opposition. And where there are centre-right governments, these tend to be lead by Christian Democratic parties - which support a mild form of social conservativism and embrace welfare state policies - that really are centre-right on the political spectrum (from a Conservative Party perspective, Christian Democrats are at best, almost like the Liberal Party, and at worst, leftist Papists).

The neo-liberal academics and pundits state that the works of Karl Marx are also a failure and should be ignored as the rubbish that they are. Again, this needs to be questioned. Marx was an economist, a historian, a philosopher, a political scientist, a sociologist, and a political activist. Of his works, what are most remembered are his works of political science (e.g. The Communist Manifesto and Capital) and that political emphasis bleeds through into his other works; this is because Marx viewed Industrialism as the dominant and most society-changing economic system of his time and thus the political, social, and economic relationships of this system were thrust into the foreground. There are indeed flaws in the work of Marx, but the majority of these flaws are rooted in the level of knowledge that existed in the 19th Century (in other words, he was not alone in this failing and his opponents of the same time period - and those of today who draw upon theoretical foundations frozen in the

temporal amber of the 19th and 18th centuries - are equally
flawed).

What was the centre of the matter, according to Marx? That
economic systems are, at their foundations, relationships between
the means of production (everything that goes into creating goods
- the resources extracted, processed, manufactured, transported,
distributed, the money or capital used, etc. - except for the
labour) and the society that they exist within. Within
Industrial Capitalism there are two classes, the bourgeoisie (who
own the means of production whose income is based upon that
ownership - therefore they technically do not have to work, they
can hire others to do the work for them) and the proletariat (who
work the means of production and sell their labour - physical and
intellectual - to the bourgeoisie in exchange for
wages/salaries).[3] Marx claimed this relationship between the
classes was exploitive because the proletariat are never paid the
full value of their labour - this gap is, in part, where the
profit comes from. Okay, I think that is enough to work with for
the purposes of this piece…

So what did Marx predict? One: he predicted that the
circumstances of the proletariat (the 16 hour day, 6 days a week,
for less than $1.00 per day, and living in cramped and filthy
slums) would, over time, continue to deteriorate until it reached
a point where the proletariat would rise up, overthrow the
bourgeoisie, and take control of the means of production,
creating a classless socialist state. That the bourgeoisie would
never permit any reforms (keep in mind that at the time that in
most of industrial Europe, unions were illegal and in some
nations the organising of a union was a capital crime) and that
the only way that the proletariat could improve their lot would
be to unite as a class and have a revolution. Two: that capital
would, over time, become more centralised and the ranks of the

---

[3] Marx also had the sub-classes of the petty-bourgeoisie (small scale owners
and self employed) and the lumpen-proletariat (unskilled and uneducated
labour). Max Weber was one of Marx's near-contemporaries who strongly debated
Marx's classes; however, Weber does not negate Marx, he argues that Marx's
categories of class in an industrial society are incomplete. Weber is often
misquoted as an anti-Marxist in American political thought - this is due to
bad translations, misquoting, and cherry-picking - which is erroneous; Weber
was critical of Marx, but not an anti-Marxist.

bourgeoisie would shrink; that the bourgeoisie would gobble each other up (economically) over time and that there would be a consolidation of capital.

So, Prediction Two was on the mark; this is 100% what has happened and continues to happen worldwide. Marx was right. Prediction One, not so much; there are two factors to consider here - the Marx factor and the union factor.

The Marx factor is that Marx was not just an academic and theorist; he was also a political activist. His theory may not have gained the prominence that it did had he been content to sit back and just discuss this theory with fellow academics. But no, he was involved in spreading his theory in the fertile environment of the Industrial Revolution. Plus, his was one of many forms of socialism that existed (and there were the anarchists too) but Marxist socialism gained ground on the basis that it was not linked to a particular denomination of Christianity or to a particular variety of philosophical thought, it was supposedly objective and scientific.[4]

The union factor was linked to the Marx factor through fear. The growth of all forms of socialism during the 19th Century created fear among the bourgeoisie and (like the present) those highly paid members of the proletariat who manage and operate the means of production for the bourgeoisie - after all, there had been the Paris Commune, and calls for radical overthrow of industrial capitalist governments, and the literature (especially the drawings and cartoons) published by and for the socialist reader that depicted these elites being disembowelled and hung from the streetlamps by their own intestines. And fear of outright socialist revolution produced a climate of grudging compromise or negotiation on issues like wages and working conditions. In the 1870s the first legislation is passed that legalised unions (or at least decriminalised unions). However, legalisation did not mean acceptance. All the way up to the 1950s there have been strikes in industrial nations where the police or military were called in to bust the strike and weapons were used on unarmed strikers. Certainly, prior to WWII in the USA, it was still

---

[4] Not really; but certainly more objective and scientific than the other forms of socialism at the time.

dangerous to organise unions; the Pinkerton's Agency used to proudly declare that they regularly killed (usually by that old American favourite of lynching) union leaders - as part of promoting their firm - hire us to deal with your pinko commie striking workers.

Nevertheless, working conditions, wages, benefits, etc. did rise during and after WWII and throughout the Cold War. It gave rise to the oxymoron, in Marxist terms, of the middle-class worker. So the second prediction of Marx did not come true, yet (we'll get to that in a moment). However, everything was heading in that direction Marx had predicted until the elites and governments (after all, the government is supposed to represent the people too) fearing revolution or civil unrest, allowed for reforms. However, getting half of your predictions correct and the other half partially correct (Marx did state what would have to occur for his first prediction to be incorrect; he just didn't accept that the bourgeoisie would ever be willing to compromise and allow for modest reforms to industrial capitalism as a probable event) does not equal a total fail. This is also why the works of Marx are still examined to the present day.

When the neo-liberals talk about the failure of Marx and the failure of socialism, what they are really saying is that the 20th Century variants of Marxist theory (Leninism, Maoism, Stalinism, Trotskyism, etc.) and the state socialist systems that they advocated and/or created failed. And that is true, but only partially true. While these Marxist variants may not have succeeded in creating any classless societies or workers' paradises, they were very successful in creating some valid critiques to industrial capitalism. I will focus on one of these critiques as it is relevant today - it is also been deemed a failed theory by neo-liberal, upper-right quadrant of the political spectrum folks; I shall briefly discuss Imperialism by Lenin.

In brief, and not to do the work justice, Lenin states that classic colonialism created the means by which industrial capitalist colonial powers could soften the effect of exploitation of the proletariat at home, by exporting the harshest forms of exploitation to their colonies. This created a "labour aristocracy" back in home countries that was insulated from feeling the full extent of capitalist exploitation and alienation. Lenin called this the highest stage of capitalism and predicted that it would be the final stage of capitalism (he believed that WWI would, upon its conclusion, lead to the end of colonial empires and thus increased exploitation of the proletariat in the industrial homelands). He was wrong there, in part.

What happened after WWI was the transition from classical colonialism (where you physically occupied the colony nation and had expenses such as colonial administration, military, etc.) to neo-colonialism (pioneered by the USA and the foundation of their "empire"). In neo-colonialism, if you control the economy of a less powerful nation-state, or the key exports, you don't have to physically occupy it; you don't have all those extra expenses and can often work out a deal where the neo-colonial nation-state pays you to have one of your military base on their soil (for their protection). Lenin didn't see neo-colonialism coming, so he was in error. However, as the developing world continues to develop, there have been impacts back in the developed nations as those manufacturing (and other jobs) move to the developed world (where they can engage in 19th & early 20th century labour practices, with little or no environmental regulations) which has resulted in the de-industrialisation of the developed nations and increased unemployment and under-employment. So, old Lenin, on this one is partially wrong, and partially right, and we'll just have to see what happens down the road.

This is a long and drawn out chaotic mess of an editorial, but I will make the attempt to bundle it into some sort of a conclusion. The central point I am making is that regardless of what our powers-that-be state, what our media says, what the tame academics and experts do claim - socialism and the works of Marx are not failed theories, are not failed political systems, and should not be (and are not) consigned to the rubbish bin of history. That the "victory" of industrial capitalism is a temporary one (we can only hope) as it is an unsustainable and unstable economic system that will, eventually fail - and fail very badly when it does. Even state socialism has had some triumphs, and while this is not a preferred system (by me; I don't care too much for vanguards, dictatorships of the proletariat, or totalitarianism); it is a system that could better address the global problems that we are currently ignoring, far better than industrial capitalism is capable of.

At some point, in the next twenty years, we will have to face those global problems and we will have to make major changes to our global societies if we are going to save this technological global civilisation. And when it comes to that task, industrial capitalism (centred on competition, hierarchy, inequality, etc.) is "just in over its head" and will have to be discarded. With hope, it will be one of the democratic forms of socialism that prevail.

So, to each and every one of us - even the bourgeois reactionaries - on this pale blue dot we call Earth; Happy May Day, comrades…

Thrashing Trufen: The Way the Future Isn't

Neil Williams

Way, way back, to be precise 33 years ago, I wrote an editorial for SWILL #4. This editorial lamented that the political views of the SF of the 1940s and their hopes for the future, were not present in the SF of the early 1980s. Upon re-reading, it is very obvious that the reading of Pohl's The Way the Future Was must have been relatively fresh in my young brain. Nevertheless, much of what I ranted about in that editorial remains true today, altered slightly, but still relevant. And so, where do I begin...

Perhaps, I should start with what type of future do we want?

From most science fiction, it would seem that we want a future not too different from right now, just with more and better gadgets. You want your flying car, mind-internet interface, easy-peasy nanotech, some bioengineering (you that your life is extended), and tame AI to do the tasks that you think you are too important to do. So you just zip out to the mega-mall to consume, etc. in what is still some sort of capitalist economy except that everyone appears to work as hard as the average doctor, lawyer, business executive in a daytime soap. Yeah, that is just some escapist, comic book-like, daydream. Any of these changes are going to have a major impact on society as a whole, both positive and negative - i.e. nothing is going to be really similar to the present.

What would I like to see; what type of future do I want? There are many things I would like to see, but at the top of my list is World Government. We really need this and the sooner the better.

Now, I realise that on all sides of the political spectrum, there are those who strongly oppose this idea, sometimes for rational and sometimes for irrational reasons. For example, the conspiracy theories that world government is a leftist plot to establish global communism or that it is an elite/corporate plot for world domination, that it is a secular-humanist plot, etc. ad nausea... The fact is (and that is why all these conspiracy theories are flowing on the internet) that we are moving in this direction anyway. Like it or not, the world is stumbling toward political integration, in a two-steps forward, one-step back, a jump to the left, and a step to the right, stuttering fashion; we don't exactly want to do it, but we are being pulled or pushed in that direction by the forces of our own making.

Right now, the world is completely dysfunctional. Image that you lived in a neighbourhood, where everyone is armed to the teeth with walled yards, and some people can afford better arms and security devices than others. If your neighbour is playing their music too loud, you machine gun their home (and hope that they don't have superior firepower to lay waste to you, your home, and your family). This is not the type of neighbourhood that people live in (in Canada) and this is not the type of neighbourhood we want or tolerate in this country and in most[5] of the developed world. No, we have restrictions of what weaponry individual citizens may own and we have police and the rule of law - however imperfect that may be, it is the preferred way to live over the armed camp perpetual warzone.

But, internationally, we live in that dysfunctional neighbourhood. And it is time that that changed. Not just because of the waste of warfare, but also because we have serious global problems that cannot be addressed in our current state of a massively dysfunctional global society.

So, what can be done?

Fortunately, a plan does exist. It is only partially worked out in detail and that is because, those finer details require serious negotiation and discussion between the nation-states, and that hasn't happened yet. So what is the plan?

It is the UN Parliamentary Assembly. This would create an extra body to the UN that would act as a "house of commons" with the General Assembly being like a "house of lords". Note to Americans: there has been little involvement by the USA in this discussion - USA governments have been in total opposition - and most of the work in this area has been done by nations who have a Westminster or Westminster-like parliamentary system, and the proposed changes reflect this.

---

[5] USA as the exception where this is de jure tolerated to some extent (and is how paradise works in the eyes of the USA Libertarian Party).

So the Secretary-General is the head of state, with powers similar to that of a Governor-General in Canada. The General Assembly would operate like the UK House of Lords or the Canadian Senate; each nation having a single seat and the representative appointed by the ruling government of the particular nation-state. The Parliamentary Assembly would be composed of elected representatives (on an agreed upon formula, more on that later), like a Westminster-style legislative assembly. Initially, the Parliamentary Assembly would have consultative powers to the General Assembly and, over time, more power would be transferred to it and its councils and commissions (ministries and departments) until it was the major governing body of the planet; the Security Council would also be phased out and abolished during this transition.

The formula for electing representatives to the Parliamentary Assembly is one of the bones of contention. China and India are in favour of a pure representation by population; this would give these two nations a majority voting block, so that formula is not going to happen. When the USA does speak on this issue, they make it clear that they will only support a one nation, one seat formula (which would render the entire exercise of a Parliamentary Assembly as futile). So, the only formulas that would be acceptable by the majority of the world's nations would be one of the weighted systems that balance representation by population with annual contributions to the UN (wealthier nations pay more) - some of these weighted systems also include factors such as the level of freedom, number of years as a UN member, and so on, but rep by pop and UN contributions are the two major factors.

Nevertheless, it is a workable system, with international precedents, e.g. the European Parliament. Is it perfect? Nope; then again, nothing is perfect. And there would be bumps and stumbles along the way, that is for certain. And it would not be utopia, or even utopian; it would be pragmatic and rational and would provide us with better tools to resolve the global problems of our age. And we would still have problems and issues; there would be regions of the world who would be winners and others that would be losers, some intrusion of the UN into the sphere of domestic politics (Russians would be pressured not to discriminate against gays, Saudis would be pressured to increase the status of women, USA would be pressured to reduce the amount of arms their individual citizens possess, China would be pressured on human rights, Canada would be pressured to properly address the issues of aboriginal Canadians, and so on). I'm not

14

saying that this would be perfect and that everyone would be happy with it all of the time and all will be absolutely wonderful; I am saying that it would be better than what we currently have. Just for a moment, think about what could be accomplished if there was a way to address global issues, if there was the rule of law worldwide, if the trillions spent annually on arms could be spent elsewhere.

A world government, as proposed via the UN Parliamentary Assembly, while it is a difficult task, is also an achievable goal. Peace and love, espoused by many of the world's religions and by the hippies way back in the 1960s, would be great; though this is not immediately anywhere on the horizon. However, tolerance and co-operation (with degree of justice and fairness) -- that we can do (if we choose to do so); it is, after all, how many of our current nation-state democratic governments work.

And for those readers who wonder why a petty bourgeois anarchist is advocating for more government, there is a method to the contradiction; perhaps then there could be an actual social evolution that leads to a political evolution without all the mess of an actual revolution. And if not, then it is pragmatic; when the social revolution comes, there is only one government to be overthrown.

Pissing on a Pile of Old Amazings

...a modest column by Lester Rainsford

Ah, ~~spe~~ splendid. So much Old Stlye Thought in the last <u>Swill</u>.
Comrade Lester is here to correnct you and reeducate you to Think
New Model Thought (the Only Thought You ~~s~~Should Be Thinking). You
capitalist rnning-dog revisionists you.

Taral: TL;DR. Your extended ap9ologia fro inappropriate
historical revisionism is noted and dismissed without deemed
worthy of a critical criticism. There is only one past. It is
clear. Do not muddy the ~~water~~ past, or the biting fish of the
pond of ideologically pure water will bite your fingers off and
pluck your eyeballs out. Promise.

Taral and <u>Chairman Swill</u>: get a room already. yhour petty
squabbles block the dialectical unfolding of necessary and self
efident class struggle.

Lloyd: points deducted for ~~reading comprehension~~ an unfortnate
tendency to misread Comrade Lester. Comrade Lester did not say
that science fiction was obsolete. Lester ~~d~~ said that some SF was
obsolete, and other SF was irrelevant. Llloyd, are you a part of
the bourgeouis reactionary anti-sicence-fiction tendency? Be very
careful, or things will go seriously with you. The camps are not
full, and due to the gloriously clear thinking of Comrade Lester,
there will always be spaces open for comrades who need some ~~e~~
additional enlightement.

Ah, so, irrelevant SF. ~~Les~~ Comrade Lester denounces the so-called
bhourgeois western "Mil SF" as being irrelevant to the clear
progress of people's SF. Perhaps at some time in the
prerevolutionary past there was some relevance to "Mil SF".
Gordon Dickson in some moments of class consciousness did examine
the military mind and the evolution of the human state to a
higher level of social organization. However, you take your
Ringos and your Webers and your runnyng dog Lackeys, and you have
trash designed to mislead the proletariat and opiate to the
masses of oppressed.

There is no "science fiction" in "Mil SF". It's a formula.

Your protagonist is a great military mind. Therefore everyone at the academy hates them, except for a couple of loyal sidekicks. The academy authorities have it in for your protagonist, and there are class enemies who are enemies in the class because of their higher class and jealousy. (This part actually hews to Correct Thinking. It is an exception.)

Your protagonist knows exactly how to fix things to make the world run correctly, but of course it is a counterrevolutionary, reactionary model straight from the bourgeois imagination.

At some event or another, your protagonist has to take control because everyone else is struck dead. Your protagonist shows an individualist genius in resoliving the situation. Your protagonist is not rewarded for this; or, actually, is rewardced by more hate and malice from the so-called privelidged eilte class.

Your protagonist then goes out and struggles in their commands, grudgingly given. This is because they are not part of the great egalitarian people's space navy, but rather some oppressive instrument of the repression of the people. So maybe this is a good thing. However, your Ringos and Webers and running dog Lackeys make it out to be a bad thing, which shows just how much reeducation they need (a lot, a very very lot).

The SF masses must be freed of this probagandist opiate and made to read Correct Thought. Mil SF is only written to obscure the class struggle and categorical imperatives of true right-thinking thought as given by the Great Steersman.

Note, Rosemary Kirstein is NOT writing about the Great Steersman. SHe too is very ideologically impure. ~~Lester~~ Comrerade Lester denounces utterly and without hesitation.

You have been warned.

Flogging a Dead Trekkie:

Violating the ~~Taboos~~ Norms of Science Fiction

Part 6 of 8 – Truly Hard Science

Neil Williams

Malzberg's Taboos of Science Fiction or in my terminology, Norm Violations. These are story concepts and/or plots that if written -- if the norms are violated -- are unpublishable; no professional editor in the genre will touch these stories with a three-metre pole, and certainly would never, ever publish them.

NORM VIOLATION FIVE: Truly Hard Science

'Science fiction truly at the hard edge of contemporary scientific investigation..."

Most of what is called "hard science" science fiction really isn't. As both Lester and I have discussed in recent issues of SWILL, there may be advanced nanotech and AI, etc., but a lot of this is not truly hard science -- there is a lot of handwavium and baloneium tossed in the mix. I have also over the years discussed the problem that much of the "hard science" science fiction, while it may deal with cutting edge discoveries in physics or biology, often becomes very soft and mushy when portraying the human social systems of 200 to 1,000 years plus into the future; so I have stated that they are only partial "hard SF".

Writing science fiction on the actual frontiers of current scientific investigation (as opposed to the fringes, which is more tolerated) can raise the hackles of both the reader and the editor -- preconceived notions are challenged. Both, may flinch and respond that the story in question is "unscientific", i.e. heretical, and therefore unpublishable.

Nevertheless, both readers and editors are probably more open these days than they were back in 1982 -- they have to be, because of the pace of change in technology and in the sciences. Nobody can keep up with everything going on in science and the less you attempt to keep up with current advances, the greater the probability that you will label the present cutting edge as being, "that-just-can't-be-right". I cannot speak to the cutting edge of physics or any of the other natural sciences, but I can speak regarding the cross-over from genetics to my field, anthropology -- in particular, physical anthropology.

It used to be that new evidence within human palaeontology would follow a punctuated equilibrium model; new data would emerge in fits and starts with periods (years to a decade) of stasis. That is because, the prime area for making these fossil discoveries was in Africa, and best within selected areas of Africa (that allowed for absolute dating techniques to be used), and it was expensive, sometimes closed off (due to civil war/unrest). There was also a certain amount of luck involved. Ideally, you set up your field camp after the local rainy season is over and see what has eroded out of the rock from the previous season. Often, you would successfully add to the catelogue of animal species already known to inhabit the region in that time period, but yield no new human or hominid fossils. And other years, there would be significant finds that would set off debate and further research.

Genetics and human palaeontology has changed all that. We are now making genetic discoveries at a much more rapid rate than fossil discoveries. Here are some of the things that we have learned over the past four years, most during the past year and one half...

As SWILL readers have probably already heard (after all, if it was reported in the Hamilton Spectator, it would have been reported in your regional news outlet) we now know that modern humans and neanderthal interbred. Contemporary modern human populations whose ancestry is from outside of Africa (in particular, outside of sub-Saharan Africa) carry up to 2%

neanderthal DNA. This was first reported in 2010 and has sparked
a hot debate between the lumpers and the spliters (lumpers who
claim that neanderthal is a subspecies of Homo sapiens and the
splitters who maintain that neanderthal is a seperate species).
As there had been some fossil evidence of admixture
(interbreeding) prior to the genetic findings, I was already a
lumper on this issue, supporting the taxonomy of Homo sapiens
neaderthalensis for neanderthal and Homo sapiens sapiens for
modern humans.

But it gets muddier yet. There are now the denisovans, who we
know more about genetically than through the fossil record, who
interbred with both neanderthal and modern humans. Homo sapiens
denisovanensis reside primarally in Asia extending west to the
Near East, Homo sapiens neanderthalenis in Europe and the Near
East, and Homo sapiens sapiens in Africa. But, there is also
another sub-species or species to add to the mix, unknown archaic
human DNA within the denisovan populations. Big question marks,
with no clear answer.

Add to this the more recent evidence that neanderthal and modern
humans share hidden DNA. What that means is because both
populations are so similar, the same DNA is indistinguishable
between the two populations (by present DNA testing techniques).
And that north-western European populations may have up to 40%
neanderthal DNA, most of that being hidden DNA.

But there is more... Over the past four months it now appears
that all of the variation between modern humans, neanderthal, and
denisovans may be due to epigenetics. This would imply that they
are all the same species and that different sequences of genes
were switched on or off between populations.

And the final spanner in the works, indirect evidence that the
unknown archaic human DNA found within the denisovan populations
(up to 5%) may be that of Homo erectus. So, if the standard
definition of a species is that of organisms that are capable
of interbreeding and producing fertile offspring; where do we
draw the line? Especially as modern humans, neanderthal,
denisovan, and erectus were all contemporaries up to 145,000
years ago?

Then there is the "Little Foot" controversy. Is this fossil a member of the genus Australopithecus or is it Homo? Is it 2.2 million years old, or is it 3 to 3.5 million years old. This will take a long time to settle (kind of like the old days in palaeoanthropology) as, based on present techniques, there is no viable DNA to extract and because the fossil is from South Africa -- fossils are more difficult to reliably date from this region.

And new evidence, keeps coming in every four to six months. It is an exciting time in human palaeontology, but it is also a messy time.

My NORM VIOLATION FIVE story draws upon all that current excitement and mess and has the working title, "All Our Kin".

Scribbling on the Bog Wall:
Letters of Comment

Neil Williams

As I write this, there is one LoC from the usual suspect (Lloyd) and an uber-long LoC from Taral. My comments are, of course, in glorious pudmonkey.

1706-24 Eva Rd.
Etobicoke, ON
M9C 2B2

March 28, 2014

Dear James:

Many thanks for the newest pile of Swill, issue 22. There is always something to say about it, and who knows, it might even be complimentary! You rolls the dice, you takes yer chances. Let's see what happens.

And with this roll, you get; whoo-hoo, State Socialism! Congratulations, comrade...

The more I see the adventures of trufen fandom, the more I find myself edging out to the outside of things. This started happening to me pretty well as soon as we retired from con-running, and many saw this as our gafiation and eventual disappearance. Well, as I've said, you don't get rid of us that easily.

We like to say that we've been kicked out of our own house by those we let in, as if we were the original tenants. As always, we forget our own neofannish days when we were the newcomers.

There are generations of fans before us, and with some luck, there will be generations after. All we can really do is add to fandom what we can, take out of it what we can, and leave it to carry on in whatever form it takes as the years go on. Fandom is a social construct, really nothing more, which as you say has split into various interests within science fiction, and the idea of fandom has been applied to non-SF properties, too.

Oh no, you have used an actual social science term of social construct (or socialist constractaliciousexpedialidocus in trufenese). Yes, fandom is a social construct and different groups of fans do construct it differently – the greater the diversity, the more parallel social constructs...

I enjoy going to some panels, as it is a slightly controlled conversation with those with whom you share that particular interest or idea, and I used to offer myself as a potential panellist. I don't do that anymore, mostly because I came to the conclusion that my experience was so out of date that I really had nothing to offer to any panel discussion, or would be chosen to be on any panel. Besides, these days, we really can't afford cons any more. We plan to be at Ad Astra for the Saturday only, so see you in Richmond Hill.

I enjoy doing panels. Though, after three years, I am beginning to run out of ideas for new panel topics. I have also learned that just because I like a particular series/film/author and read all their books/seen all the episodes does not make me knowledgeable on that topic. The true fan of the series/author has done that as a starting point and then read every article published, the author's entire blogsite, etc. I will remain open to being on panels, though...

The locol…I have read that when many long-time SF readers get tired of SF, they will often move over to murder mysteries/suspense/detective fiction. I've actually taken a break from reading as a whole, and I am not really missing it. I know that sounds heretic, but perhaps that's just an indication that I have had enough, at least for a while.

If I had to read a myriad of EQAO literacy tests, I would want a break from reading too. I have on occasion read some mystery fiction, but I tend to find it more formulaic than most SF & F. Once I find an author I like, they rarely write completely different stories in each novel - they will often focus on a particular "detective" or setting and thus after book three it starts to get a little dull. Of course, I also have my academic reading when I want a break from SF…

Disorganization at Ad Astra…it just comes down to people not willing to put the effort they put into their professional jobs into their volunteer jobs, especially the ones they take on with Ad Astra, or any other convention for that matter. As an example, this year, I got in touch with Ad Astra three times, asking for dealer information, to see if we could run our steampunk table there. I never did get the information, so we figured, that's okay, there are other conventions we can be at to deal, so we have tables at the upcoming CostumeCon and Anime North.

The past three years of attending Ad Astra, all I can say is that it is disorganised. Polaris may have been just as disorganised internally as Ad Astra, but on the surface (for the individual dealer, panellist, attendee) it certainly appeared to be organised.

We're all too human in that we want things to stay the way they are, just as we like them. But many of us are in our 50s, 60s and even 70s, and we may share that desire, but that is more a function of age than things changing around us, and a function of other people changing your fandom until it is unrecognizable to you. Taral mentions OSFiC a number of times here, and while it was meant to be Toronto's local SF club, Yvonne and I were never members, and after all the politics we heard about, we never pursued memberships. We may have asked at one time, and were refused admission…that was a long time ago, and there has never been another club to come along that was a general SF club, no matter what any of the local Trek clubs thought.

Other than the fragmentation and the wide array of SF media, a lot has not really changed over the past 30 years in several ways. General cons, like Ad Astra (and formerly Polaris), have both literary and media tracks in their programming. Even SFContario, which appears to have been founded as a small literary convention, has substantial media programming. The amount of SF & F released in all mediums every year is staggering in comparison to 30 years ago and this has been accommodated and has also, in part, been a major factor in the fragmentation of fandom.

There are a greater number of women visibly involved in SF & F fandom than there was decades ago. There is a greater visible presence of GLBT persons in fandom today, than in the past. Both of these changes are positive developments. Nevertheless, SF & F fandom, who attend fan-run conventions, do, for the most part, appear to be an over-35, European-descent segment of the population.

In repeated conversations with the under-30s, it would seem that this whole geek-culture thing is just a generational re-branding of all things SF & F. There is a generation gap (probably gaps if we include sub-generations) in lingo and in expectations. The under-30s want more experiential, participatory, customised programming in the fan run conventions. Their idea of a how a panel should run tends more towards that of the parliamentary scrum than a moderated colloquium (depending on the sub-group – some would prefer the "talking stick" forum). In brief, there is no one, single fandom anymore.

And therein lies the dispute with Taral (and his fellow travellers) who only consider the type of fandom that existed when there was a single fandom, as actually being fandom.

Ah, OSFiC... Regardless, as to what Taral continues to say, OSFiC was not the most welcoming and inclusive of organisations, which, to compare it with a general SF fan club of the same time period, BCSFA actually was. Both claimed to be provincial clubs and both were really just Toronto and Vancouver clubs (at the time). BCSFA is still around and, on paper looks healthy; OSFiC is extinct.

Based on your comments to Taral, the next issue should be interesting. Let's see if he comments, or ignores you. Either may happen…either way, I am looking forward to that next issue. See you then, but before then, see you at Ad Astra, about a week away now.

Yours, Lloyd Penney.

Sorry Lloyd, but no fireworks for the LoC Column. While Taral did not ignore me, his comments were NFP. Let us just say that, for now, we agree to disagree. He does actually respond to me in other fanzines (e.g. Space Cadet) though. Good to see you both briefly again and again at Ad Astra. My next con will be SFContario in November – and there will be a SWILL party…

It has been a long time, since I have written at all about science fiction or for the fandom of science fiction; it is too depressing, as is the future. But, I saw a picture of you wearing soviet t-shirt on Facebook and that makes me smile. This is not the future imagined in 1980s. Today is a capitalist dystopia science fiction nightmare the whole wide world. Trotskyites said that Soviet Union was "state capitalist". You called it "state socialism", but you are a petty bourgeois anarchist individualist and ideologically incorrect. Your state tolerates your beliefs because they do not fear you. Without vanguard of the proletariat there can be no success, no revolution, no challenge to capitalism. Capitalism has won. Today is grim the future even more dire.

Russia is capitalist, for now. Putin was KGB. Who knows, he may bring back the old ways. Is possible with Eurasian Union plan. I miss the Soviet Union.

Seeing picture of soviet shirt gives me hope. This I thank you for.

Nazdrovia.

Vladimir Schnerd

Comrade,

Always great to hear from an original SWILL contributor. Yes,
I am still ideologically incorrect and I did wear a Soviet t-shirt to
the event you refer to. Perhaps all is not as grim as you think…

As for Comrade Putin, read on…

Endnote: Back to the USSR?

Neil Williams

While I do not have any longing for the USSR (like Comrade Vlad),
there are times when I do actually miss the Soviet Union. Not
the purges, the totalitarianism, the gulags, the restriction of
freedoms, but I do miss there being an ideological adversary to
the USA. I do miss there being a check and balance to USA
imperialism. And, who knows, Comrade Vlad may get his wish from
that other Vlad, Vladimir Putin.

It has been 22 and one half years since the dissolution of the
Soviet Union. And that dissolution has been chaotic in part.
The USA and the NATO nations did not rush in a reconstruction
plan for the former Soviet Union as they did for Western Europe
after WWII (ah, but that reconstruction aid was to prevent the
spread of "communism"; silly me...), but instead opted for
imposing Milton Friedman's economic shock therapy on Russia and
the former Soviet republics. A bully-boy tactic of kicking one
when they are already down (and a perfect example of the sore
winner). So, what Russia got was massive privatisation of their
assets (aka structural adjustments), a tight monetary policy,
lifting of price controls (as part of liberalising trade) and
hyperinflation. This created an instant depression and business
oligarchism (some legitimate businesses, others criminal, and
many a bit of both), and government corruption. Not admirable.

While there has been improvement over the past decade, there
remain problems in the Russian economy and in the government.
There may be a freer economic market, but there is massive
government and corporate corruption, and not a substantial
improvement in individual freedom. Nevertheless, for the past 13
years I have been telling my students that at some point, Russia
will get its act together again. And when that happens, it will
be a force to contend with. That is starting to happen.

Russia, in its own words, has been "left in the corridor" by the
USA and the European Union (and Canada) over the past twenty
years. Russia has been left out and thus has decided to go it

alone in the "if you can't join them, beat them" philosophy. And
so, the Eurasian Union is born. Although an economic union,
there would seem to be a subtext of a deeper political union,
e.g. the Union State that already exist between Russia and
Belarus. Putin has stated that the Eurasian Union would embody
the "best values of the Soviet Union". The USA has dismissed the
Eurasian Union as "re-sovietization" or as the "Neo-Soviet
Empire".

Now, I do see the Union growing and perhaps most of the former
soviet republics will join (not the Baltic states or the Ukraine,
though the later will have lost Crimea and possibly south-eastern
area historically known as Novorossiya to Russia). Will this be
a new resurgence of the Soviet Union? To early to determine. It
will be a union, it will be more authoritarian than the European
Union and the democracies of the West, and it will remain more
socialist than the USA and Canada. Will there be a return to
Marxist-Leninism? I wouldn't bank on it, nor would I rule it out.

Putin is a former KGB officer who took part in the 1991 hard-
liner August Coup attempt and only switched sides when the coup
went sour. And looking at the United Russia Party, it carves a
sort of middle road in the centre that rejects state socialism
and fascism, while at the same time retaining structures similar
to that of the old Communist Party of the Soviet Union. It is
more probable that we will see a Eurasian Union, that is no more
democratic than its current members, with a mixed economy
(socialist and free market), that is at best Western-neutral and
at worst hostile. I wouldn't call it a new Soviet Union, but it
would have Soviet Union aspects.

Who knows, it is not yet the 2020s -- Ken MacLeod could be right
-- maybe the Eurasian Union will re-institute Marxist-Leninism
and the old name too...

On Names and Things

Some of you may have noticed that I have changed my name, yet
again. I have discussed things with the Union lawyer and it
would seem that the corporate running dog reactionaries of HR at
my place of employment cannot make any claim on my actual birth
name as I have not used this at my academic institution. And,
since in the fanzine community, the keepers of fannish history,
have declined (possibly for the sake of continuity) to use my
current legal name, preferring my old unmarried name, I will use
Neil Williams for my fannish writing.

Fiction and unapproved academic work will be by **James William
Neilson** and employer-approved academic work will be under **Neil
Jamieson-Williams**.

This is probably as clear as mud, but welcome to corporatised
Canada...

Pith Helmet and Propeller Beanie Tour

November 2014   SFContario 5 -- Toronto

SwIll

#24   Summer 2014

Table of Contents

SWILL is published quarterly (Spring, Summer, Autumn, and Winter)
along with an annual every February - in other words, five times
per year.

SWILL

Issue #24   Summer 2014

Copyright © 1981 - 2014 VileFen Press

a division of Klatha Entertainment an Uldune Media company

swill.uldunemedia.ca

Editorial: Star Trek Sux

Neil Williams

Yes, I did say that. Just to make it clear (especially for those
Trekkies with an overabundance on fat intermixed with their brain
cells), I will say it again; Star Trek sucks! In fact, Star Trek
sucks shit!

There, now I have done it - I will most certainly face the Wrath
of the Trekkies. Not that I really care; SHRUG, they're only
Trekkies...

Oh, and don't get all, but I'm a Trekker not a Trekkie... Look,
if you actually believe that you must attack any criticism of
this media franchise, that no negative words must ever, EVER be
spoken/written about Star Trek, then you ARE a Trekkie. For you,
this television programme has become something akin to a
political philosophy/religion -- a worldview that must be
defended at all costs from all detractors, perhaps even unto
death... This also means that you are beyond reason, beyond
dialogue - and from the Trekkie POV anybody who has not drank
the Kool-Aid and bought into the belief that all things Star Trek
are sacred is Other and The Enemy. You will hate everything that
is said in this issue (and you will do so without actual thought
or any reasoned reflection).

For my second heresy; Star Trek (in all its forms) is just a
media franchise centred on what was just a television programme
that first aired almost fifty years ago. It IS only a television
show...

What are the major strengths of Star Trek? Three of the more
common defences of Star Trek that Trekkies usually trot out are,
that in Star Trek there is (are):
*   actual scientific speculation
*   serious subject matters
*   an optimistic future

There are obviously more than these three, but this is enough
material to deal with for purposes of this editorial.

In Star Trek there is actual scientific speculation. Yes; and
no. It all depends upon the context being used. In comparison

with its USA television contemporaries (Voyage to the Bottom of the Sea, Lost in Space, The Time Tunnel, The Invaders, Land of the Giants) then, yes, Star Trek is superior in its scientific literacy and speculation; superior, but not excellent, and certainly not perfect. However, if the level of actual science in your competitors, e.g. Lost in Space, is abysmal, being superior to them doesn't make you wonderful, it just places you above being a scientific illiterate. Face the facts, in all incarnations of Star Trek, there remains a substantial amount of science and technology that is pure baloneium, i.e. pure unadulterated bullshit; but, as long as it is not so absolutely, outrageously wrong or it does not require over a minute of techno babble to create the illusion that it could be considered to be plausible, we let it go. This does not mean that Star Trek is "hard science" or on the forefront of scientific and technological speculation, it only means that it is somewhat more scientific than its American television contemporaries.

Now, if we compare Star Trek to print medium science fiction of the late 1960s, it doesn't look superior at all. It is simply military (albeit a mild variety) space opera, good space opera, but space opera nevertheless.[1] It is a 30% Royal Navy of the late 19th Century and 60% the American Navy during World War II and 10% the American Navy of the 1960s. Oh there are aliens, i.e. different cultures, most of whom are humanoid and can interbreed with humans,[2] but most are not that different from our cultures - and Trek never does (being on broadcast television) create cultures that are analogues of some of the more different cultures (for example, cultures where homosexuality is the norm) that have existed or are still extant on our planet. And then, there are the alien cultures that are just mirrors of Earth history - allowing for the use of pre-existing costumes and sets - such as Romanworld, Naziworld, Gangsterworld, Aboriginalworld, Westernworld, etc. What ever happened with the First Federation - which was older and more technologically advanced than the United Federation of Planets - but only appears in one episode in all of the Trek series?[3] What of the many other near-equal to the United Federation of Planets species that also have a single

---

[1] Star Wars - the other megafranchise - is fair to poor space opera.
[2] Yes, I am aware that this was supposedly sorted in a Next Generation episode - but it is a weak solution in my opinion and has holes (except for the believers).
[3] Yes, I do know that this species was further developed in novels and computer games - I am just focusing on televised Trek (the medium that the franchise was created in).

walk-on episode and are never heard of again?[4] And finally there are the adversary aliens in the original series - the Klingons and the Romulans - or should I say the Soviets and the Chinese vs the Federation aka the USA.

Look, if this was a story or serialised novel published in a SF magazine back in 1968, it would have been criticised as being hack space opera - even by most Analog readers of the period (though not by the most "rah-rah USA" military SF readers of Analog). While, the later series (I am going to be really, really kind here and not even make mention of the Trek films, any of them) do attempt to rationalise the canon (when they are not violating established canon) and do attempt to make the Federation appear to be more pluralistic and more democratic and less militaristic, Trek still does not come close to matching the good to excellent in print SF.

Star Trek dealt with serious subject matters. Sort of… Yes, we have the first people of colour in positive roles on USA television in the original series and we have the first inter-racial kiss on USA television, and so on. But were there actual serious problems examined in the television programmes? Yes, there were at times. And where those problems handled seriously; most of the time, they were not. Usually, Star Trek approached these problems as fables and morality plays. And I have no actual problem with that; there are strict limits to the 50 minute (or less) episodic broadcast television format. Star Trek, especially the original series, does its moral fables and cautionary tales well for television of the time period, and I do not dispute that. I do dispute the Trekkie notion that those televised morality plays are the pinnacle, the absolute zenith of political/social/philosophical thought on these problems and issues. They are not.

Did Trek bring these issues and problems to the general USA television audience? Yes, it did to some extent. Are they the only television drama to do so? No, they were not. Did they do it better than other television programmes; in regards to the original series, sometimes. However, the closer we get to the present, the less that is so. Star Trek series have always been made for broadcast television and subject to broadcast television constraints - cable and digital television network dramas can deal in far more depth with controversial issues and social problems than what is permitted on "the USA public airwaves".

---

[4] Ibid.

Star Trek does raise the social and political problems of the day (for the time period when each series was being produced) but as episodic television, it cannot penetrate these issues as well as a limited serial (e.g. Orphan Black) is capable of doing - if they choose to do so.

Star Trek presents an optimistic future. That really depends upon your worldview, it really, really does. I am only going to focus on the original series, as it is this series that sets the foundation for the Star Trek happy-happy future. The thing is, how positive is it?

Well, you have a sort-of nice, just-so fantasy of a prosperous, harmonious world, with racial/ethnic equality (some gender equality), and no internal social/political conflicts. In essence it is an American, 1960s middle class, stepford future (the sub-text of conformity is strongly present), that still contains financial inequality, is capitalist, is militaristic, and while within humankind there is a higher degree of equality than in the mid-20th and early 21st Centuries, there remains an vertical mosaic[5] regarding other species (with humankind on the top). United Earth and the United Federation of Planets are nothing more than the United States of Earth and the United States of the Galaxy. Oh, and although humans are no longer fighting each other, that doesn't mean that we are without war -- no, we are constantly at war, usually small wars, with other species (just as the USA has almost always been at war during most of that nation's history). Plus, and here is where Trek canon is inconsistent, there have been two World Wars since WW II (the Eugenics War is sometimes referred to as WW III and WW III sometimes referred to as WW IV -- nevertheless, both are world wars and all that such global conflicts entail).

True, this is all modified in the later series, with energy so inexpensive that it isn't charged for and replicator post-scarcity economies. However, there is still a high level of

_____

[5] For Americans who are probably unfamiliar with this term, the vertical mosaic was coined by the Canadian sociologist John Porter in his examination of Canadian society in the mid 1960s. Porter describes an ethnic/racial "pecking order" that existed -- and continues to exist -- within Canada that has evolved over time. The Canadian vertical mosaic is flatter today than it was in 1965, which was flatter than it was in 1900. But, those who form our elites, those who have, on average, greater opportunities, tend (in 2014 Canada) to be those of Western European descent, with other ethnic/racial groups ranking below this group. This also plays out in Star Trek where humans are the species at the top of the mosaic, then the Vulcans, etc. down the chain.

conformity and militarism. And humankind has been perfected (I
guess that some aspects of the Eugenics Wars did get passed down
into the mainline of the human genome) which, to me, sounds more
sinister than positive. And it isn't all that democratic,
either. Military ethics trump social ethics and the Federation
Assembly appears to be little more than a parody of the UN
General Assembly and subordinate to Starfleet. Beyond the
surface, this is not a positive future in my opinion. It is a
phoney future, which has a strong friendly fascist undercurrent.
And this is but a brief, back of the envelope, dissection of Trek
society...

I think that David Gerrold said it best, "Star Trek is the
McDonalds of science fiction". That about sums it up. And most
people agree, McDonalds food sucks; so does Star Trek.

Thrashing Trufen: Plucking the Great Bird of the Galaxy

Neil Williams

Wherein the editor does continue his heretical acts upon Star
Trek, compounding his Trek-crimes and thus increasing the odds
that he shall attacked by anger-frenzied Trekkies at the next SF
convention that he attends that has a strong media SF programming
track (however, given that the average Trekkie weighs at least
115 kilos -- and most of that is not muscle -- I am relatively
confident that, even at my age, I can out-run them)...

For my next diabolical deed, I shall turn my gaze to none other
than Eugene "Gene" Roddenberry aka The Great Bird of the Galaxy.
Perhaps it would be wise to express some trepidation regarding my
intended plan to trash a personage who is revered as being at
least a Trekkie "saint" if not the Trekkie "Supreme Being", but I
won't. At the same time, as somebody who never knew the man, who
never had any dealings with him, etc. I have no strong emotions
involved concerning Gene Roddenberry; I have no axe to grind, nor
scores to settle, truths to reveal, nada, zip, nothing. All I
intend to do here is to point out the fact that Roddenberry's
human failings outweigh his alleged "sacredness" and to deny his
canonisation and/or deification -- not that that will sway any
Trekkies out there.

Primary Heresy: Gene Roddenberry was just a man, an ordinary
human being, no wiser, no more brilliant, no more noble than the
majority of us 7.2 billion who currently inhabit the planet.

Secondary Heresy: Any overarching vision that can be attributed
solely to this one man, Gene Roddenberry, was (as discussed in
the Editorial of this issue) a hodgepodge of not very realistic
wishful-thinking; a Pollyanna melange of sanitised 1960s
counterculture tropes, middle-class American norms, and rose-
coloured, fairy-glamour, just-so projections that are a patina or
veneer that hides, upon actual reflection, a darker societal
structure. Sub-Heresy: of course, Star Trek was created not as
great art, but as a throw-away commodity (as are most television
fictional programmes). Just like fast food, it is the initial
taste that matters, not the nutritional content -- similarly for

Star Trek, the vision is to be consumed and actual thought is not required. Roddenberry was not a good philosopher, nor a good sociologist, nor a good futurologist (or even a good writer) - though he could be viewed as a good, not above average or excellent, television/film producer (and even then, he had failures intermingled with his successes).

Tertiary Heresy: Complementing my Primary Heresy, there is ample evidence that Gene Roddenberry was not just an ordinary human being, but that he was also not a very good ordinary human being. Well, he was a television producer for USA broadcast network television; while there may, just may, be some saints amidst this peer group, they are very, very rare (and Roddenberry was not one of them). A brief list of his failings would be: he was a womaniser, unfaithful husband, may have committed sexual assault against one of the female cast members on the original series, was an absentee parent, occasionally stole material from writers, manipulated contracts to deprive actors, writers, and composers from receiving the full royalties/residuals due to them, required actors to provide him a "cut" of any outside work they did as a Star Trek character, and made outrageous, false claims that served to build the inflated effigy of the god-man Roddenberry.

Since the death of his second wife Majel Barrett-Roddenberry, there have been several "tell-all" books that have been published by Trek insiders (and others) -- so don't just take my word for it (though take the Trek memoir books by Shatner with a kilo of salt -- these are ghost-written anyway). Roddenberry, when alive, was also very inconstant on the version of the tales he told about Trek. When not speaking to the faithful, Roddenberry does state that he drew inspiration for Star Trek from A. E. van Vogt's *Voyage of the Space Beagle*, Eric Frank Russell's *Men, Martians, and Machines*, C. S. Forester's Horatio Hornblower novels, and the film *Forbidden Planet*. But, when speaking at Trek conventions, there are no outside influences or inspiration, Star Trek emerges whole from Roddenberry's mind and he is the sole, singular creative force behind the series.

Another great inconsistency, which is very well documented (so well documented that I shouldn't have to mention it), centres on the episode *The City on the Edge of Forever*. According to Roddenberry; Harlan Ellison turned in a mediocre first draft script, that was going to be too expensive to shoot, had 'Scotty dealing drugs', and had to be re-written by Roddenberry to 'save the episode'. This is 100%, complete and absolute chickenshit rubbish -- i.e. it NEVER happened. Let me repeat, NEVER, EVER

happened.   Again, check it out for yourself, the original
teleplay was published in 1976 in *Six Science Fiction Plays* ed.
Roger Elwood and again in 1996 by Ellison in *Harlan Ellison's
City on the Edge of Forever*.[6]   And yet, Roddenberry continued to
tell this lie at every Trek convention he attended.   And of
course, Roddenberry's version continues to mouthed as the
Dialogue by the numerous priests and priestesses of the Trek-cult
and the lumpen-laity -- the Trekkies -- parrot the whole lie back
as the Response in some kind of prayer to "Saint" Roddenberry.

Gene Roddenberry was a human being with human failings who was
the producer for a television show called Star Trek; a programme
that was good space opera for the time period, and that's all.
Roddenberry was no saint, no bodhisattva, no demigod (though he
had a huge ego and probably perceived himself as such, especially
when being worshipped at Trek conventions) and all the claims of
the Trekkies that he was "holy" (and still is) does not make it
so.

And I will continue to speak these heresies, even if I should
find myself before the Trekkie Inquisition...

---

[6] In brief, very brief, because there are some people who are too lazy to
check primary sources. All of the writing/production staff (Roddenberry
included) loved Ellison's first draft of *City* -- nobody thought it was sub-
standard or mediocre. It did run over budget, but not $100,000 over budget as
claimed by Roddenberry and his followers (probably more like $50 - 60 k over).
However, budgeting (unless one is a showrunner or writer-producer) is not a
writer's responsibility; budgeting is what production staff does (in
particular the line producer). In the original version of the script, the
character Scotty, does not appear at all in the episode; yes, there is a
crewman dealing drugs but it is not one of the main cast. Roddenberry never
re-wrote the script at all (though he definitely had someone put in some
stupid dialogue), the script was re-written at least twice by the series
writing staff. Ellison himself, in the failed attempt to maintain the
integrity of the original script while also pleasing Roddenberry and the
network, did at least three re-writes of the script for no additional
compensation. Roddenberry did not rewrite *City*, nor did he save it - he did
have others do the re-writes and the final shooting script was of far lesser
calibre than the original. If you want more details and are too cheap to buy
the book, sign up for one month free trial on Scribd and actually read *Harlan
Ellison's City on the Edge of Forever*.

<u>Pissing on a Pile of Old Amazings</u>
A ᴴModest Column by Lester Rainsford

A couple of weeks back Lester spotted, from the comfort of his seat
on the Queen streetcar, a tall and gangly Spock hanging out on the
corner. Sure, this was Queen West, and was Spock really that tall,
after all he couldn't be taller than Kirk could he? The sheer ego-
force of the universe should prevent Ꭵthat possibility.

At one time, long ago, Lester would have been excercised by this. The
world was new, mediafen gorged on Star Trek and Star Wars and The
Empire Strikes Back were polluting skiffy as we knew it. Fat trekkies
charged around convention centres, threatening all and sundry as if a
herd of red-shirted buffaloe were on the stampede.

Now, things have changed. Lester sees no need to cling to the
verities of the past. That he leaves for nostalgic truefen with
delusiins of SMOFdom. Sometimes we need a reminder of how things are
changed--see in a run-down TTC subway station all the empty
boothettes for pay phones, and remember when pay phones were
everywhere. Likewise, mediafen have gone off to their own mediacons
(by and large). Star Wars brought forth Jar Jar Binks who is not to
be unremembered. Skiffy has been taken over and ecliped by fantasy,,
and crappy extruded-product multivolume extreuded product at that. SF
cons are now sedate, as all the greying ᴍᴀᴍᴦᴀᴀᴋᴍ (hmm, 'con-goers')
take their Geritol and are asleep by nine PM, assuming they have
stayed awake through the panels in the first place. A bit of mayhem
would not be a nuisance, it would be a welcome sign of life.

As for Spock on a stretcorner, if Lester's eyebrow rose in Ꭵ the
Vulcan manner, it was only the barest of twitches.

But Lester ᴍᴋᴍᴍ <u>does</u> have something co complain about. A couple of
things.

First of all, there is the "Star Trek reboot" which contains what are
allegedly junior versions of Kirk Spock et al. The movie is filled
with gratuitous explosions. Worse, Kirk is played as some kind of ADD
Mozart as seen in <u>Amadeus</u>, all shit-eating grin. Whatever kind of
prodigy the young Kirk may have been, he wasn't this. Lester was
disappointed that no ᴋᴋᴍᴋ Salieri was availabel to poison the
grinning little shit. Lester wathed this on a cottage-sized old-style
tube TV. The cottage owner is a Star Trek fan and loved the movie,
hence Lester had to view it all the way through, no way out. Didn't
loke. Wouldn't recommend.

Then there is <u>Redshirts</u> by Scalzi, which won some awards or
something. Lester read this recently. The opening reminded Ꭵ Lester
of Stoppard's Rocenkrantz and Guilderstern are Dead. This apparently

occurred to a lot of other readers of taste and discernmenbt. There is a difference, though. Stoppard ends with Rosencarntz and Guildenstern bneing dead. Scalzi does not allow this logical outcome in Reshirts, starting with a goofy deux ex machina of this old guy hiding in the engineering spaces. Okay, the guy isn't a deus, but ex machina sure holds. Then, having written an all-round unsatisfactory engine, Scalzi throws in two codas that for some readers were the true apotheosis of this book.

Lester begs to disagree, having been left with the kind of raised eyebrows that an ersatz Vulcan didn't. As Scalzi tried so spin out the fix, the logic of the situation got murkier and murkier. Van Vogt would have handled it without any problems (it was Nazis from the secret moonbase you see) but Scalzi is no Van Vogt and Redshirts is no Slan. Frank Herbert came to mind, but that's unfair to Herbert.

What Scalzi pulled in the last part of Redshirts was a Piers Anthony. Anthony has a way of (sometimes) coming up with a good idea, but then not being arsed to figure out all the implications and dealing with the most obvious contradictions. So it starts interesting, and devolves by the end of the book into half-hearted armwaving.

Scalzi has been accused of being a facile and perhaps lazy writer, and Redshirts shows both bad aspects. Stoppard may be facile as well, but R&G are Dead is a clever tour-de-force, so the reader is motivated to ignore the facility. Not so with Redshirts which should have been one-third the length and ended badly for the redhirts, or at least existentially. Having taken on more than he can reasonably explain, Scalzi then gets laxy and does a terrible job of explaining just how this removed-by-time=and-space television show remote-control character patterning works, and how the redshirts can weasel out of their predicamenht. None of the logic that was presented made any sense whatsoever.

Stoppard didn't drag Shakespeare on stage to explain Hamlet, never mind give R&G anything but RXXXB an existential despair at being trapped in their roles with no exit.and Scalzi sholdn't have tried to drag Shakespear onstage either. What should have ended badly for the redshirts ends badly for Scalzi and awards voters. There's a lesson in there somewhere. Perhaps ASpock can figure it out; it's too much for Lester!

Flogging a Dead Trekkie:

Violating the ~~Taboos~~ Norms of Science Fiction

Part 7 of 8 – SF About SF

Neil Williams

Malzberg's Taboos of Science Fiction or in my terminology, Norm Violations. These are story concepts and/or plots that if written -- if the norms are violated -- are unpublishable; no professional editor in the genre will touch these stories with a three-metre pole, and certainly would never, ever publish them.

NORM VIOLATION SIX: SF About SF

"Science fiction which questions science fiction; work which questions the assumptions of the category and speculates on the effect it might have upon its readership..."

I really don't have too much to say about this. There are very few professional published stories/novels written that break this norm. Is this because editors and readers view the violation of this norm as more than norm violation but as the actual breaking of a taboo? Possibly. It could also be that there is so much of this type of story that is published unprofessionally (for example, faan fiction and much of fan fiction).

One could say, for Trek fans (and others), that Scalzi's Redshirts is an example of the violation of this norm. (Lester has mentioned this novel in his column and I agree with his analysis, such as it is...). But this norm-breaking novel was professionally published -- which would support that this is not a norm violation. Then again, it is parodying Trek, which means that it is not questioning the assumptions of science fiction as a whole nor the impact the genre has on its readers/viewers, only

Star Trek. And there have been numerous Trek parodies over the decades and one feature film (Galaxy Quest) many of which were written by Trekkies themselves.

And the question has to be raised, is it possible to write a story today that criticises and/or calls into question the entire genre and those who consume the genre that would be seen as a norm violation by everybody, including editors and publishers? I can't answer that; I would speculate that it would be a difficult task to accomplish. Even the most anal retentive defender of all things Trek is not going to be upset by Redshirts (as Scalzi gives himself and the reader wiggle room as the novel is about a SF series that is a bad knock-off of Star Trek), because the Trekkie can pretend that Scalzi is not really questioning Star Trek itself. With so many mediums today in the genre and the proliferation of subgenres and sub-subgenres -- how can one write something that will enrage all of fandom enough that an editor/publisher will not publish it? I don't think that it is possible.

It is possible, to violate this norm for specific audiences, but not for the entire audience. Say, if within Redshirts it was made blatantly clear that this novel was all about Star Trek, Scalzi would have enraged the Trekkies and would be receiving hate-mail, etc. However, I doubt that fear of Trekkie wrath had anything to do with this decision though the potential of legal wrath from Viacom would have been a strong consideration.

With the vast diversity in the genre today and the massive amount of faan and fan fiction out there on the web and elsewhere that consistently does violate this norm (though not in professional publication), a writer is going to have to be very clever and very original for such a story to be published. Otherwise, the editor is just going to go, "Meh, I read something with a similar idea on a website last year (poorly written, but the same idea)." And they will pass on the story, but not because it broke a norm.

So, what about my story? It is a noir-themed alternate history where the Futurians back in the late 1930s early 1940s won the battle to control fandom and SF had strong socialist/communist themes. Until the 1950s when SF was viewed as an "un-American activity" and there was a Magazine Code (like the old Comic Book Code) and the genre in the USA was sanitised. The Cold War is still ongoing but it is now a cool war (the 1991 hard-liner coup in the Soviet Union was successful) and US SF is either military SF, happy engineer tales, or pure space opera. Real SF exists outside of the USA; F & SF is published out of the UK, Galaxy and If out of Toronto, etc. And the US government continues to place pressure on the Canadian government to halt the flow of contraband literature from crossing the border, physically and electronically. The Canadian government does not consider this to be a high priority and does the bare minimum to appease the Americans on this issue; they sub-contract P.I.s to track down the distributors of this material. The story centres around one of those P.I.s in Hamilton, Ontario.

The story title is *Subversive Stories*; it has already been rejected twice. So, maybe the violation of this norm does still have consequences...

Scribbling on the Bog Wall
Letters of Comment

Neil Williams

As I write this, there is one LoC from the usual suspect (Lloyd).
My comments are, of course, in glorious pudmonkey.

1706-24 Eva Rd.
Etobicoke, ON
M9C 2B2

May 16, 2014

Dear James:

Or Neil. Happy Day. There, that covers them all. Thanks for Swill
23, and must make some comments on what I've seen. Habit of mine.

Well, I am a little confused as well... We have a tentative
agreement (the details have yet to be released) which may
change things regarding my name. Plus we have a new
President at the College so there may be positive internal policy
changes...

Buncha Wobblies, hm? When I see the abuses of internships and
other forms of unpaid labour, unions are needed more than ever. I
also see reports of constructive dismissal through having your
own job's description rewritten, and then suddenly not being
qualified for your own job. I was dismissed from an agency-based
job, and then I reapplied, I was told I didn't qualify for
it, the job I'd held for eight months previously. Unions can be
dangerous, but for the most part, they provide services to stave
off the abuses of the workplace.

The current abuses are many. Re-writing of job descriptions being one of the newer management fads. I disagree that unions can be dangerous, unions serve to improve the workplace and employee compensation (in both salaries and benefits); if the union is not doing this, then, it is time for the membership to vote in an union executive that will. "Buncha Wobblies" -- sure, I ltake that label (although I am not a member of the IWW)...

Yes, Comrade Lester, I am a part of the bourgeois reactionary whatchamacallit, but with SF tendencies. I have hacked into the Federation transporter complex, and will be willing to beam over any number of antimatter buttons anywhere you might be. A GPS spot has been beamed directly into your epidermis, and we can beam a button into your person at any given time. Now THAT's serious, and a little enlightenment. :)

I cannot speak for Lester, but your ideological stance has been recorded and you are, indeed, a bourgeois reactionary apologist and class traitor. You are hereby sentenced to mandatory re-education -- for Trekkies the re-education centre is located on Tantalus V (you must find your own transportation and pay all transportation costs).

I have never enjoyed military science fiction, but I can see where it came about. who else but the military, especially the American military, could have the funding to build the ships to take humanity to the stars? I've read elsewhere such dreams to go to space in such force an American wet dream based in the Cold War. (We all carry up to 2% Neanderthal DNA? I can think of several people where that percentage is much higher.)

I have on occassion read military SF, but this subgenre has no strong draw. The politics are almost always right-wing authoritarian with an almost obscene love of guns, guns, and more guns... The USA military has had grandeose plans for space (at least in Earth orbit and the Moon on paper (perhaps they still do) during the Cold War period. These never materialised, and perhaps never will, which is fine by me. As for the stars; not bloody likely unless super cheap FTL is developed...

Oh, I am pretty certain that I have more than 2% Neaderthal DNA, my ancestors are from Mid-Wales one of the regions in the UK that has the highest frequency of archaic human DNA (ie. Neanderthal). So, I wouldn't be too surprised if I had up to 10% Neanderthal DNA.

We did go to Ad Astra, but only for the Saturday. We did have some fun, but through seeing old friends, and going for some shopping in the dealers' room. I did get the feeling from one or two committee members of "What are THEY doing here?", but as long as we pay our $$, we can go and enjoy ourselves. (I reminded them that of all the people I know, Yvonne is the only local fan to have attended EVERY Ad Astra.) CostumeCon 32 was more fun, not only because we were vendors, but also because we saw friends we hadn't seen in decades, we knew many of the other vendors there, we did about $550 of business there, and we soaked in an atmosphere of creativity and appreciation. As I type, the weekend after the long Victoria Day weekend is Anime North, and we have a table there, and hope to do some good business. (With all this capital business discussion, I have totally blown my cover as a bourgeois reactionary. Whoops.)

Yes, you are petty-bourgeoisie and undoubtably a reactionary. Off to re-eduaction with! As for Ad Astra... SHRUG, you paid your membership, therefore you can attend. It is not for the present con-runners to question the attending of con-runners past. (They should be sent for re-education as well...)

A question. I think I figured out a while ago why my own
interests have changed as they have. Maybe it's a mid-life
crisis, I don't know, but at some point, I stopped looking
forward to the future with optimism (as a science fiction
reader), and started looking back to the past with nostalgia
(as a steampunk fan). Is there a particular reason for a change
like that? Is this something a lot of people go through? I don't
think this is such a strange thing to do, for I have changed
interests in the past before, but I just don't know when it
happened and why. I may never find out, or there might be some
interesting psychological reasons that happened.

Ah, I touched on this many issues ago, I am certain. One: it is
getting harder to write a near future story that doesn't get dated
within a couple of years due to the pace of technological change.
Two: yes, the current future trends do look bleak. And so, there
is alternate history SF (including steampunk), steampunk
fantasy, more fantasy, and far future SF in response to these two
facts. On the flip side, we have the endless YA dystopias,
Singularity booster wet-dreams, and detective/police fiction set
in the very near future... In general, there is not a whole lot of
hope out there right now and that is being reflected in the
fiction. If the mood changes, so will the trends in fiction -- or so
I speculate... I wouldn't call it a mid-life crisis but for someone
who is a self-professed Trek fan it is an example of deviant
behaviour -- you too could find yourself before the Trekkie
Inquisition.

All done! Off it goes, and I am slowly getting caught up a huge
pile of zines I wanted to respond to. Hope you and your merry
band have a great long Victoria Day weekend.

Yours, Lloyd Penney

Endnote: Disruptor Cannons Ablazing...

Neil Williams

Whaaa! You have dissed Star Trek and the Great "God" Roddenberry. You have destroyed my illusions. Don't you know how much Star Trek means to me? Don't you know that Star Trek gives my life meaning? Don't you know that Star Trek saved my life? What kind of mean, heartless, sicko are you? Whaaaaaaa!!!

The kind of mean, heartless, sicko who would write, "edit"[7], and publish SWILL -- it is a very "strong fit", as the HR saying goes, for SWILL. Odds are, you have never even heard of SWILL, nor what the focus of this zine is, until someone on the Meath Park Star Trek Lives Blog posted a link from the Outer Wawa Trek Forever forum about this dastardly attack on all things Trek and a link to this particular issue. So, you don't know SWILL and you don't know me (or Lester for that matter).

Look, if Star Trek saved your life, or gives your life meaning, and if what has been written in this issue crushes that meaning; it couldn't be very strong to begin with.

Whaaaaa, you're any even bigger bully!

Really? So, I tracked you down on the internet and somehow forced you to read this issue; that would be a bully-tactic. But that didn't happen, did it? No, you were told that this issue was anti-Trek, you decided to read it -- all by yourself -- and you are now complaining about it.

Here is what it is really like to be bullied. (Note to regular SWILL readers this is a recap from a previous issue...) When I in my last year of primary school (first year of middle school had we remained in Quebec) my family moved to Ontario. This was the time period where the FLQ still existed and there was strong separatist sentiment in Quebec and the view from the rest of Canada was that Quebecers, all of them, were whiney, ungrateful, traitors. Especially in the regions of Ontario where, at this

---

[7] As regular SWILL readers will have noticed, I do very little editing of the zine content. Only social media content is subjected to some editing.

time period, the Orange Lodge still had some influence. You see,
we were Roman Catholic[8], and we had arrived too late in the year
for my siblings and I to be enrolled in the Catholic School
Board, we had to go to the regular public school. And so, I was
called a "frog" and a "traitor" and occasionally a "papist" and I
was beaten up every single day at school for an entire year. Not
just me against a single bully, no this would be me against all
the boys in my grade. Not only was this tolerated by the
administration of this school, it was approved of by the school
principal (an Orangeman). This was constant, persistent,
systemic bullying and one of the things that did help at that
time was that my parents exposed me to science fiction.

I would not at all say that SF saved my life or that it gave my
life meaning, but it helped, to some degree, to ease the pain.
Thing is, I started on the works of Arthur C. Clarke and if I was
a Clarke-fan version of a Trekkie, I would only read Clarke
stories and novels. I would only read works that were very
similar to Clarke. I would rant every time that someone did an
adaptation of a Clarke story or novel that it wasn't perfect or
exactly like the story/novel. I would leap into flame wars
should anybody even in subtext be critical of Clarke the person
or of any of his works. But, I don't do that. I still like
Clarke; he is "old school" but he has an interesting style, but
that style has flaws and not everything he wrote was good. I
also moved on to other authors and I really don't have a single
favourite author (though Clarke, LeGuin, MacLeod, and Hamilton do
kind of have a favoured standing), nor do I have a favourite
television series...

While there are novels that I regularly re-read (these are few)
and there are others that I have re-read just because it has been
many years since I first read them -- sometimes this can be bad
for the novel/author (I liked Niven in my teens and early
twenties, but find his work sucks, to me, today) or good (I read
most of Malzberg's key works of fiction at too young an age and I
appreciate them more today) or unchanged (I don't like Heinlein
any more than I did (i.e. not) in my youth and I still like
Spinrad). The thing is that my tastes have changed over the
years, not a huge crevice, but a definite shift and the last
thing I want to do is read the same thing over and over and over
again...

---

[8] Note to Americans; here in Canada, the majority of citizens who practice
Christianity are Roman Catholics. I'm no longer a Roman Catholic or
Christian, but I was when I was younger. They even had me Confirmed twice,
but it didn't stick…

Therein, is the problem of the Trekkie. They want the same thing over and over and over again. Just Trek, and more Trek, and yet another helping of more Trek. Yeuck!!! No thank you!

Look Trekkie, branch out a little, will you?!! Science fiction is supposed to be a literature of ideas (yes, much of the time it doesn't live up to this, but the best of it does). Science fiction is supposed to make you think and question; to ask why and what if even if the answers are potentially or actually frightening. There is a term for any fiction that is intentionally and consistently sub-standard, fiction that gives you the answers you want to hear and never really challenges the reader -- we call it hack writing. Much, not all, but much of space opera falls into this category -- the reader's norms, values, mores, are not seriously challenged or are just made slightly uncomfortable -- it provides an action adventure that spans interplanetary to intergalactic space, many worlds, many cultures, etc. But most space opera doesn't really make you think or question any more than the latest major box office hit action film does. And neither does Star Trek, most of the time, and when it actually does do so (try and make you think or question), it then blows it with some technobabble or platitude-based eleventh hour solution that makes everything all right and wonderful (which never happens in the real world).

Whaaaaaaaa! You're mean!!!!

Hey Trekkie, look ever here. WHACK! That's a slap to the head. Look, there is a great big universe of fiction out there, even if you just stay within science fiction -- strange new worlds, new civilisations, new writers, new universes that you can boldly explore... Or, you can remain within your Trek box, absorbing a steady diet of the TV dinner of fiction and endless reruns of Star Trek past. So yes, please stay in your self-imposed prison and throw away the key...

And fuck you too.

Pith Helmet and Propeller Beanie Tour

November 2014 SFContario 5 -- Toronto

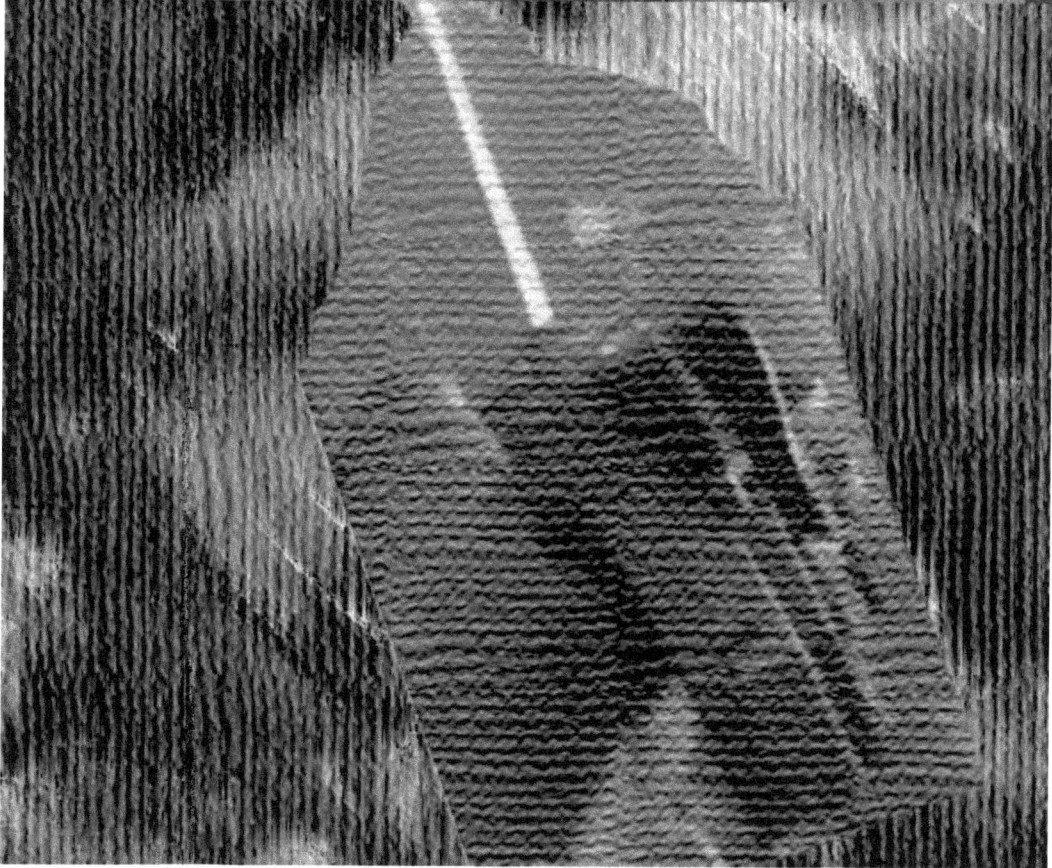

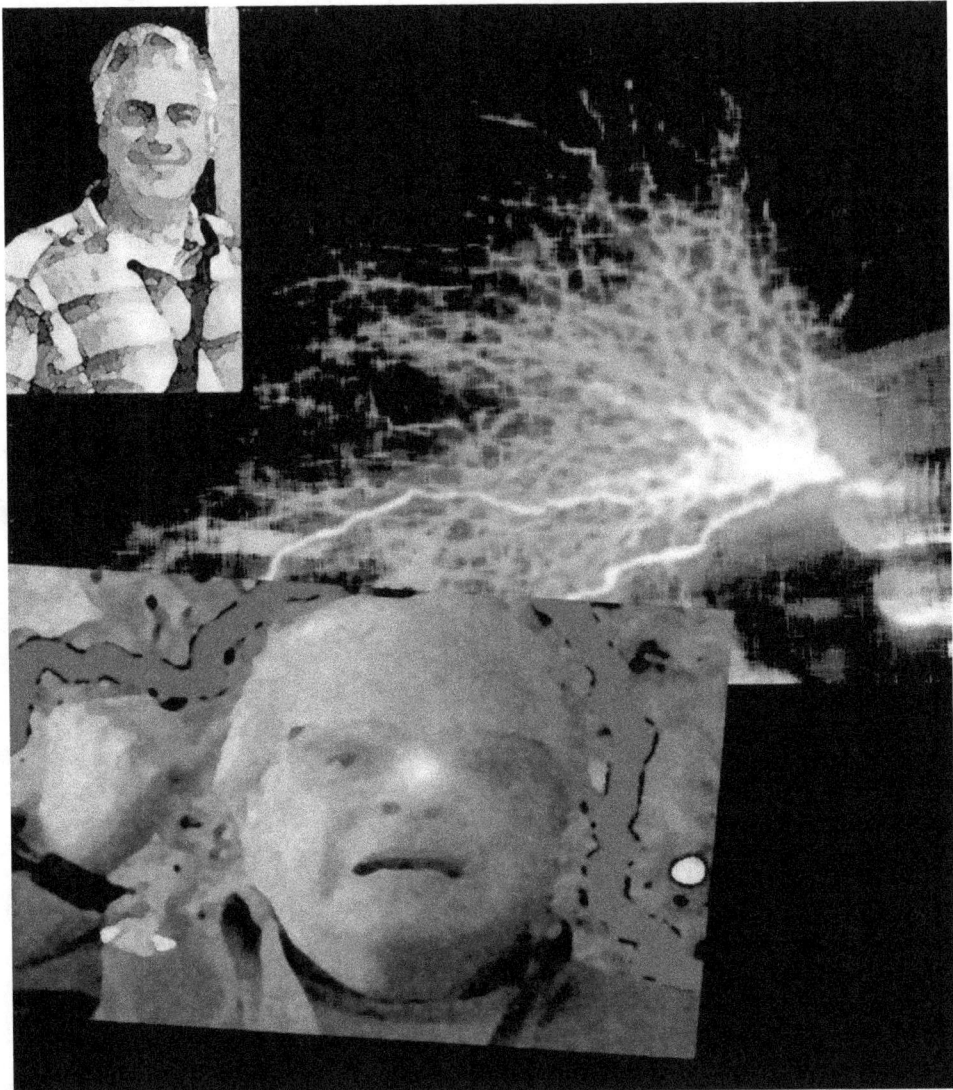

#25   Autumn 2014

Table of Contents

SWILL is published quarterly (Spring, Summer, Autumn, and Winter)
along with an annual every February - in other words, five times
per year.

SWILL

Issue #25 Autumn 2014

Copyright © 1981 - 2014 VileFen Press

a division of Klatha Entertainment an Uldune Media company

swill.uldunemedia.ca

Editorial: ~~Tolchocking~~ Baiting Ellison

Neil Jamieson-Williams

We Interrupt This Programme For the Following Announcement:

In March 26th, 2014 I decided that in keeping with the unannounced theme-arc of SWILL 2014 -- that of norm violation and attacking sacred cows - that the Autumn issue would be an anti-Ellison issue. On October 10, 2014, Harlan Ellison ® suffered a stroke, which was announced in the media on October 12th. Even I, the evil anti-fan editor, did consider changing the planned autumn "trash Ellison" issue, due to his illness. However, as the updates continue to come in, it would appear that Ellison is recovering well, that his mind has been unaffected, and that his physiotherapy is making progress - and, he is already writing again. As this is the situation, and, after all, as this is SWILL, there is no longer any concern, on my part, that I am kicking-someone-when-they-are-already-down. This is not as mean-spirited as it sounds; unlike the other victims of SWILL in 2014 (e.g. Trekkies and "trufen"), Ellison - even when partially physically incapacitated - is a target that can hit back and hit back with a venomous bite. I truly and honestly (really honestly) wish Mr. Ellison a continued and rapid recovery. I have held this issue back, just to make sure that Ellison's health continues to improve. It has and winter is almost upon us. That being said, the show must go on; here is the Autumn 2014 issue of SWILL…

We Now Return to Our Regularly Scheduled Programme, Already in Progress:

... it's a rather futile task, or one that does evoke a certainty of failure; so, be it. In a truly quixotic fashion an attempt will be made to tolchock Ellison -- knowing full well that the attempt will probably fail. However, SWILL has always been very adept at prodding at soft spots and pushing buttons in the past[1] and so "baiting" would be the more appropriate editorial title.

---

[1] less so these days (perhaps it is because I am no longer in my early twenties when there were many issues that I viewed as polarised black-and-

However, in this case, there is a potential danger -- one does not exactly know what may be invoked by this issue of SWILL. I may call forth a demon that could consume me - I am treading on the tail of a tiger, which in all probability will maul me and eat me. SHRUG. And yet like the Tarot deck Fool, I go onward.

So, what am I going to hit Ellison with? That is the big question, indeed. The the crux, the foundation, the centre of it all is that I have respect for this man's work -- both fiction and non-fiction. He is a brilliant writer, intelligent, with biting wit, etcetera, etcetera, and so on... I like a lot of what he has written over the past fifty five plus years, and some of what he has written I have hated, and some of it was just okay; the majority though, I have liked, and some of his work will be remembered long after his passing as 20th Century literature in the short story form. Ellison's work has been an influence (but just one of many influences). Just to make it clear, I am not a fan -- i.e. not an Ellison fan, someone who worships every word that emerges from his manual typewriter or the man himself.[2] I neither deify nor do I demonise Ellison -- he is just another human being, who happens to be, in my opinion, and excellent writer of short fiction. However, there are a few malenky items that I would like to deal with; that Ellison is an uber-misanthrope, has a slight tendency toward "yellow journalism" in his essays, that he is a Yank, and has been documented to have behaved as an arsehole. And that is more than enough to play with in this editorial. And I am going to use the shotgun approach, where you just hope that some pellets will strike home and stick.

When it comes to being a misanthrope, Ellison is one. Although he likes to attribute this to the influence of Mark Twain, this is not an apt comparison. Twain did work with and made use of misanthropic themes, but, he was not a misanthrope. Twain still liked humanity and held the belief that if humankind could just free ourselves of the notions that we were hand-crafted by some divine being and that we should await our reward in the next life that we would make substantial steps to improving ourselves, ourselves. Both Twain and Ellison are atheists -- I am not --

---

white-issues and also because of the fragmentation in the spec-fic supra-genre that makes it very difficult to piss off everyone).

[2] As I have stated in previous issues, I have no single favourite author in speculative fiction. I have a major "pantheon" which includes the eclectic mix of Clarke, Leiber, LeGuin, Malzberg, MacLeod, Moorcock, Sheldon, and Spinrad -- Ellison resides in my second tier...

though I agree 100% with both of them that if you take the position that the universe and this small planet were created by, and watched over by, and ruled by a divine being, then the only logical and rational conclusion is that "God is a malign thug."

But, Ellison goes further than Twain does with this. Ellison takes the position that humankind, the entire human species -- at the core -- is little more than scum; a mean-spirited, moronic, venal, blood-thirsty, lazy, greedy, blight with no redeeming qualities that are worthless and should be eliminated as the living waste products that they are. With one exception (which is so typically human; that there is at least one exception to a universal, and that the single exception is also self-serving) -- those within the human species who are creators, in particular the makers of art.

Uhmmm... Does he mean all creators (which would include scientists, inventors, as well as artists -- and could also include economists and financiers, and that is now very problematic) or does he just mean artists? And how is this defined, exactly. Who is making these grand decisions as to whom is a creator or an artist? Is it society (that has a tendency to not recognise creators and artists for their true worth during that person's lifetime)? Is it the creative/artistic establishments (which are, of course, never, ever wrong or biased)? Is it the will of the people (not bloody likely, given Ellison's views on the average person, and again, a collective not known for having any better track record than society as a whole in judging creativity and art)? Or is it just Ellison, himself?

First of all, are we, as a species, mostly just scum? Not really. I am not making the argument that we are noble, or moral, or ethical, because, we aren't. And anyway, it is we, the human race, that have created these many codes of nobility and morality and ethics -- codes that often conflict with one another. We are primates, we ARE the third chimpanzee, with some of the worst aspects of Pan troglodytes and perhaps a bit of the best of Pan paniscus mixed into our unique melange of a genome. I am not making the "cop-out" that biology is to blame, but I am saying that it is a definite factor that has to be considered.

We also have to look at our societies and cultures. Looking back over the past 10,000 years, we can say that most of our societies sucked and I would speculate that many also sucked prior to the Neolithic Revolution. But things did go downhill once we develop agriculture; inequality (economic and gender), hierarchy, authoritarianism, imperialism, slavery, religious dogma, and so on… On the other hand, agriculture did pave the way for the emergence of what we call civilisation - writing, metallurgy, architecture, engineering, medicine, the movable-type printing press, industrialisation, etc. Wonderful benefits and terrible consequences. One could blame society for why we are the way we are. A strong case could be made here; after all, for the past ten millennia most of us have lived under authoritarian rule (democracy is a rare and precious thing amidst civilisation and one can argue that democracy is actually antithetical to civilisation). But, this position is also a cowardly attempt to weasel out of responsibility. Nevertheless, society is a definite factor to be considered.

Or are we to blame, each and every one of us; including me, including Lester, including Ellison? Well, we are. We do not take the time, we are not involved, we are too wrapped up in our own problems, we just want to survive, maintain what we have, get by, and maybe get a little bit more, and have some level of comfort. This is not, in of itself, evil - though it can allow for evil to flourish. And this is also an easy answer that blames both the perpetrator and the victim equally. That easy American answer (more on that later) that it doesn't matter if you were born to privation or are a trust-fund kid, you both have equal opportunity to succeed, if only you self-actualise, or seize the day, or think positively, etc. It does contain some truth, but not the whole truth, and it is also an evasion.

However, there are no simple and easy answers. Each of these three factors play a role in why we are what we are; imperfect, fallible, at times reprehensible, at other times wonderful, and entirely human.

And part of being human is being creative and artistic.

Now, I do agree that what is created, the art itself, may be absolute shite. It may be over warmed, re-processed, naive, below sophomoric, moronic, derivative garbage -- it may be pure swill -- but we are all capable of some level of creativity. And some of us possess an innate talent above the average, and many of us possess the average that can be improved by practice and dedication to achieve a degree of excellence, and some of us were doled out a below average serving of creativity that still could be built upon. And just because one is a brilliant musician does not mean that that same person can write creatively. And many of

5

our creators, and our artists, are only mediocre at best, and yet, they can still make a living perusing their art -- they are not famous, or rich, or outstanding in their art, but they do support themselves via their creativity. Should only our best creators be spared and the rest be sent to the re-education camps, the gulags, or into the arms of the death squads?

If Ellison had been granted the powers of a god, or even that of a demi-god, the answer to that question would be, "Yes." And, he would have already laid waste to nearly all of humankind.

My second issue with Ellison is that, at times, there is a hint -- and at other times a stench -- of yellow journalism in his essays. Yes, I do realise that these are, in the majority, polemic, opinion pieces and should not be treated as if they were actual detailed analyses on a particular issue, topic, etc. I do fully understand that these are not academic articles in even the loosest definition of the term. However, when the author of these opinion pieces condemns the lumpen prols for not having an informed opinion, for not checking facts, and then proceeds to commit the same offence -- then the author should be held accountable.

Ellison does do this; yes, he really has. For example, in Installment 48 and Installment 49 of "Harlan Ellison's Watching" in the December 1994 and January 1995 issues of Fantasy and Science Fiction he trashes two entire generations on the basis of evidence that is simultaneously slim, biased, and circumstantial. I really don't know where to begin with here -- there is so much wrong with Ellison's analysis of what he calls the moron generation (switching back between both the Baby Boomers and Generation X and tarring both equally and treating both as being synonymous) that it deserves its own article. However, as I am just using this as an example, we will stop here and I will conclude that Mr. Ellison's informed opinion is not always as informed as he thinks that it is... (Oh, and just to ease the ego; yes Harlan, you are 100% correct, the 1994 film version of The Shadow is horrible on numerous levels and is definitely a "stupid film" -- I would add in more of Ellison's metaphors but I do desire to avoid American civil lawsuits -- I will add my own instead, it was rancid chickenshit.)

And so we segue into my third issue with Ellison, American-blinders. While, Los Angeles may be the current centre of American culture and American art, and while USA culture and art is dominant -- for now -- within the infant global culture, diffused by globalisation and the corporato-governmental arms of PillageCorp (a subsidiary of Loot&Burn R Us Inc.) and their fellow conglomerate/nation state consortiums, as they roll forth to transform the world into one big, exactly the same, suburban sprawl and power-centre complex. All of us -- who reside outside of the USA (though also within the marginalised populations within the USA) -- experience American cultural imperialism. This is not a good thing -- the homogenisation of everything -- for the world or even for the USA. Yes, it is beneficial for the interests of the USA entertainment conglomerates in that it means more profits and more wealth. But the cost, the cost is cultural loss and, to use the American term, cultural levelling. I don't think that whatever they are doing in California is the pinnacle, the zenith of human culture and I want some choice, thank you very much. And I want the choice to choose my own cultural products that speak to my experience, not the Henry Ford option -- you can have any culture you want, so long as it is Californian.

And finally, the most subjective of these issues -- is Ellison an arsehole? Well, I have only met him once, at Westercon 37 (recounted in SWILL 14 "Starlost Memories") and that was not a positive experience.[3] There are many other recollections of

---

[3] I also did some more research here as well prior to this issue. I'll add in some extra information, though the names will be omitted to protect both the innocent and the guilty. Back in 1980s, I wrote a lot of radio drama and non-fiction radio programming. I used to socialise with a small group who wrote professionally (though, in my case, not for markets that would qualify for SFWA membership - and I was also in ACTRA, out of ACTRA, in a see-saw situation depending upon the production and whether or not I was a producer, I usually was; it was complicated…) and worked in the same area of the downtown. We met every two to three weeks for drinks; there were four regulars and about six irregulars in the group. I was the only one who wrote SF, though the soft-core porn writer occasionally wrote within the borderlands of SF, and there was one of the irregulars who seemed to know a lot about science fiction but never stated what it was that he actually wrote. On the road to Westercon, I discovered that that irregular was a published SF author and that my girlfriend's best friend was his mistress - as they say, small world. So, it is on this author's vouching that I got into the SFWA suite to begin with, I didn't have the proper badge to be in there, which Ellison would have noticed at a glance, and probably assumed that I was some fan who somehow managed to crash the suite.

Ellison behaviour by many people who have known him and or worked with him that would lend support to the hypothesis that Ellison is an arsehole. I have seen him on television and in the 2008 documentary film, Dreams with Sharp Teeth; and there is evidence that Ellison is arrogant, egotistic, and some that he is a bit of an arsehole. The central issue being the definition of an arsehole; according to the Oxford, "a stupid, irritating, or contemptible person". Well, of the three descriptors, I would go with number two -- irritating -- and thus, on these grounds, Ellison is an arsehole. And thus, so is my father -- who is only three years senior to Ellison -- and who is known to make similar rants about people's driving habits to those recorded of Ellison in Dreams with Sharp Teeth (though my father, an Anglo-Quebecer Roman Catholic, would use the word "swine" or some Quebecois swear word where Ellison uses the word "motherfucker"). And, I guess, so am I -- the publication of SWILL being ample evidence against me.

In conclusion -- there isn't any. I have fired my grapeshot and we will see if it finds its mark. If it does, I guess I'll receive something in the post from Mr. Ellison's legal counsel...

I could also be that the author (not the same person as in the paragraph above) who introduced me to Ellison was a factor - I am not naming names here but, as far as I know, this author didn't publish anything past 1991 and almost of his prior output was military SF. Now, this author lived close enough to the border to be able to listen to the radio serials that I wrote when they aired and he liked them a lot. Well, he liked the universe I created, but he didn't like the political slant; he wrote the typical right of centre, authoritarian, military SF space opera and my serial was military-ish interplanetary space opera that was left of centre - the anarchists and socialists in the asteroid belt vs the big, bad corporate Dominion of Earth. Anyway, this author and I had met at V-Con and at Norwescon previously and had political arguments and still remained on a strong acquaintance-level. I did not agree with his quasi-Libertarian politics (quasi because he had a Heinleinian notion of who gets to be a citizen - Libertarian Party world for those folks and top down authoritarian rule for the non-citizens) or his views on women or his views that hunting deer with automatic weapons is still a sport (I was a hunter back then, though a bow-hunter). And he didn't agree with what he called my "commie shit". SHRUG. I don't know, I'm just giving Ellison a further out - maybe he was rude because he despised the person who introduced me.

And yes, you are going to be forced to open another webpage to see what was written in SWILL #14…

Thrashing Trufen: An Archetypical Anti-Fan

Neil Jamieson-Williams

When it comes to being an anti-fan, or in advocating an anti-fan agenda, in comparison with Ellison, Lester and I are simply pikers. While Toronto fandom, in particular the aging trufen of Toronto and southern Ontario, see us as eeevil-doers and a cancer upon the purity of fannish essence - I have to admit that Ellison has us beat, every time; even if he was strapped into a chair a la A Clockwork Orange, he'd still whoop us. Ellison is the archetypical anti-fan.

I could cite, I normally would, but there are legal questions that Canada and the USA do not agree upon regarding what is and what isn't fair use in a piece like this, and Ellison being an American (and an American who has provided ample evidence of being litigious) may decide to sue -- which is an annoyance that I don't need -- so, I will refer you, the reader to look up the examples yourself.

The evidence for Ellison being an archetypical anti-fan does require a qualifier; Ellison doesn't hate all fans, just the worst of the breed.

Exhibit One: This can be found within the essay "You Don't Know Me, I Don't Know You" wherein Ellison pillories fandom for:
- contributing to theft (of royalties/annuities) by purchasing bootleg editions of SF authors works
- believing that an author's characters are an accurate reflection of the author's personality/personality traits.
- and the elevator story -- that probably occurred at the 1974 Discon in Washington, DC -- that should be read.[4]

Exhibit Two: This can be found within the essay "Exogenesis" that tolchocks and razrezzes fandom from start to finish. Not only are there examples from Ellison's experiences, but also from many writers from the same time period -- 1984. The kernel of this

---

[4] This essay can be found in the July 1977 edition of The Magazine of Fantasy and Science Fiction or in the book Sleepless Nights in the Procrustean Bed.

piece was Ellison's guest of honour speech from Westercon 37 that was expanded upon as an essay. There is too much material to itemise here and the vast bulk of it damning and with due cause. Again, you should actually read it...[5]

> *Sidebar: As mentioned last issue, I know many of you baulk at the thought of being directed to source material -- "why won't you just tell us" -- but, you know what, fuck off. One, to "just tell you" would violate copyright (not going to do that). Two, it is good for you. If you are going to have an informed opinion, you really should actually read the source material. Yes, reading the Coles Notes for Mansfield Park because you found early 19th century English too boring, or you didn't have time, may have got you through a secondary school English Lit test, but you really didn't actually read the novel and you really don't know the novel. If you actually read the source material, you have a better foundation to base your opinion on rather than just my interpretation of the source material.*

Two exhibits are all that are needed. There is nothing that Lester or I have done to fandom in print that Ellison has not surpassed, in some instances by a few parsecs. We are mere shadows in comparison. In his wake, I wonder whether we should just shut down SWILL altogether. Ah, but who would annoy the local trufen, then. That would be an abrogation of responsibility on our part. While I cannot speak for Lester, I myself, am in awe before the master, the archetypical arch anti-fan, Ellison.

And I implore him to -- keep tolchocking fandom!

---

[5] This can be found in the book <u>Over the Edge</u> or in <u>The Essential Ellison</u>.

<u>Pissing on a Pile of Old Amazings</u>
A ꟷModest Column by Lester Rainsford

Do you know that there is <u>one</u> person in the world who ever got ripped
off by other people? Do you know that there is <u>one</u> person with the
guts and the clear-headed orneriness to declare that he got ripped
off and oppressed by the Man right in public? Do you know that there
is <u>one</u> persoℲn in the whole entire world who has held on to Artistic
Integrity when all the luddite know-nothing philistines have sold out
to mammon and convienience? Do you know that there is <u>one</u> person in
the entire universe, yea verily in the entire history of the cosmos
since the Big Bang itself, who has been hard done by and has written
about this and talked at length (and at length) and moreso has
declared that he has been hard done by, and deserves the greatest of
praise and respect thereby, to right the wrongs done to him?

Yes, Lester's modest column is ꟷꟷ <u>so</u> underappreciated.

But to hear Harlan Ellison talk about this, he is even worse done by.

Nonsense. Harlan is someone whose time has passeꟷd, long passed. His
career is as dead as Last Dangerous Visions, and his influence is
similarly dead. The only reason he's talked about thses days is
through misbehaviour and litigation. If Sꟷwill didn't talk about
Harlan, who would talk about him at all? Who would care?

Harlan Ellison should be happy to beꟷ talked about here. It's ꟷꟷꟷ the
only place that's award-winning that cares, after all.

Lester is not interested enough to go back and research if Ellision
was a true <u>enfant terrible</u> or just an <u>enfant terrible manqué</u>. The
only people who really care right now would be nodding off over their
Postum. AND IF YOu know what Postum is, you know what Lester means.
In any case, <u>enfant terribles </u>morph, with time, to batshit crazy old
guys. Harlan's a bit different from Heinlein, for example, but the
principle remains. And the onlyt people who are going to listen to
batchit crazy old guys are other old people, possibly certifiable as
well. Like <u>Swill</u> and its readers thereof.

It's all good!

But, you know, what's old is new again. Lester isn't sure how much
the past is really the past, or whether it recurs, like the Buddhist
dream (or nightmare). That seems to be the case with award-winning SF
these days. Lester will writeꟷ more about this anon.

Flogging a Dead Trekkie:

Violating the ~~Taboos~~ Norms of

Science Fiction

Part 8 of 8 – ~~Genuinely Feminist SF~~

Neil Jamieson-Williams

Malzberg's Taboos of Science Fiction or in my terminology, Norm Violations. These are story concepts and/or plots that if written -- if the norms are violated -- are unpublishable; no professional editor in the genre will touch these stories with a three-metre pole, and certainly would never, ever publish them.

NORM VIOLATION SEVEN: Genuinely Feminist SF

"Science fiction in which women are perceived to react to events and internalize in a way which is neither a culturally received stereotype nor a merely male stereotype projected onto female characters."

I, like Malzberg, am somewhat ambiguous regarding exactly what a genuinely feminist SF would be, other than to say that some of our female writers have produced examples of this type of SF. It is far easier to state what it isn't, and much of the female protagonists, even written by women, are really just the standard male protagonist with female genitalia. I am also not certain that this is a form of science fiction that I would be comfortable writing, and I have never previously, gone out intentionally to perform this task. Nor am I confident in the outcome.

Given the restrictions of the genre, and of our society, it is hard, for me, to truly imagine a real feminist science fiction. I am not saying that the task is impossible, after all, it has been done, but it is a difficult task.

I will place emphasis first upon our society, as it strongly impacts upon the genre. Even though, here in the western industrial democracies, and, in particular, within Canada, were the status of women is currently almost on par with that of hunter-gatherer societies;[6] these remain patriarchal societies. Here at home, our current federal government is of the opinion that the proper place for a woman is as a wife and home-maker (that women don't need to be lawyers, or business-people, or politicians as this would take away time from raising a family). While that political party has transformed itself and aligned itself with the USA Republican Party over the past fourteen years and is not a true mirror to the Canadian body politic, those memes do remain within our society. The present scandal regarding sexual harassment of female MPs in the House of Commons is an illustration of those old memes that possess a strong cultural inertia.

It is difficult to envisage a genuinely gender-neutral, let alone a genuinely feminist society. Regardless of social engineering, reforms, and etcetera -- it does appear that there are biological tendencies that cannot be ignored, try as we might. Yes, culture can trump biology, and does so all the time, but the biological factors don't just disappear; they remain. And, because we live in a patriarchal society, because we do not live in a gender-neutral society, it is difficult to determine what is set in place by biology and what is built by culture. Gender enculturation or socialisation begins, with our present technology, prior to birth -- as soon as the parents know the sex of the child -- and at the very latest upon birth. As the parents have not been raised in a gender-neutral society and

---

[6] In hunter-gatherer societies, most of the food supply is that which is gathered by the women of the band. Both sexes hunt small game, and the men engage in big-game hunting. However, hunting is not always successful and is always less successful than gathering. In these societies, adult women and adult men have equal status and equal say in how the band is governed. Any group of men who desire to install a patriarchal coup will be quickly stopped in their tracks by the simple and non-violent tactic of ceasing to share the plant food gathered by the women with the men -- people like to eat. Only when a culture has previously been an agricultural or horticultural society that has now adopted a hunter-gatherer economy do we see gender inequality; the status of women is always lower in agricultural and horticultural economies and this cultural trait is maintained even when the people switch to a hunter-gatherer lifestyle.

because the surrounding culture is not gender-neutral, gender enculturation is very rapid. It provides us with yet another chicken and egg conundrum.

The genre of science fiction is still a male dominated genre, even today; the speculative fiction surpa-genre is a little better, but only because the the YA market. But, getting away from the just the gender of the writers; based on context alone, there is little within speculative fiction that could be said to be feminist. And there is a large segment of spec-fic, especially in fantasy/YA fantasy, that is anti-feminist -- e.g. The Twilight series and the protagonist Bella (who is an anti-feminist archetype of the helpless, infantilised woman -- or, in this case, woman-child) and the numerous knock-offs. For all of the "strong female characters" that we now have in speculative fiction, those characters, tend not to be very feminist -- and where they are, they tend to be, at best, moderate (minor reform) feminists or anachronistic feminists.[7]

Can there be a genuinely feminist science fiction? I will say that it is definitely possible. I will say that the more the status of women increases (and we have backslid in this regard with our current government as many of the party members of the party in power believe that the proper place for a woman is as a homemaker -- preferably barefoot and pregnant, and if not in the kitchen, at least in the home -- as stated by my local Conservative MP) the more possible and probable it is for genuinely feminist science fiction to find a niche in the marketplace and a readership. Though, I honestly think that a true feminist science fiction must await the emergence of a true feminist culture (or at least counterculture) in opposition to the patriarchal global culture that we all reside within.

---

[7] So, the queen is a feminist and may extend some modest level of womens rights to her ladies of the court. But she has no intention of granting any human rights (political or gender) to the peasants -- who are not really fully human, being commoners -- or to make any changes to society as a whole. The pucky, feminist protagonist, who pulls-herself-up-by-her-own-bootstraps, to rise from the dregs of society to be Admiral of the Imperial Fleet will be a top-down authoritarian who has no difficulty with any form of authoritarian rule, be that absolute monarchy, state socialism, or corporate facsism. These are not real feminist charactors -- though they do fit the bill as strong female characters

Is it something that I could write? I don't know, maybe -- but there will remain a high level of uncertainty here... Initially, my plan when I finally got to this "taboo" was to end this piece with ambiguity and the vague promise of making the attempt sometime in the future. However, I did write a story -- a rather long story -- that is, at least feminist, though I do not think that it can be called genuinely feminist. I wrote it for an anthology[8] that wanted feminist stories, and also wanted the protagonist to be bi or lesbian. There were some other restrictions in the anthology guidelines -- and there was a key one that I ignored (which will be one of the reasons why the story was rejected) because the story required that this restriction be violated, though I had some hope that the story itself may have surmounted the restriction-violation...

At present, I am uncertain what to do with this tale. It either has to be strongly cut or heavily expanded, before it goes out again. I'm still thinking about this one... The story's working title is Welcome to the Occupation.

---

[8] For those readers wondering why some of my turn-around times are rapid and others are long, here you go, from my recent experience. Anthologies are more structured, tend to have themes, and also have slow response times. Magazines are more rapid, and the online magazines are faster still, and the flash fiction markets are the swiftest of them all (usually). For this experiment, I have also, for the most part, written these stroies with the specific norm-violation in mind and a specific anthology in mind -- anthologies have strict deadlines and I am not too good with self-imposed deadlines...

Scribbling on the Bog Wall
Letters of Comment

Neil Jamieson-Williams

As I write this, there is one LoC from the usual suspect (Lloyd).
My comments are, of course, in glorious pudmonkey.

1706-24 Eva Rd.
Etobicoke, ON
M9C 2B2

September 26, 2014

Dear Neil:

Many thanks for Swill 24. A 2-4 of Swill, and let's hope there's
a deposit on the empties. I will make sure I have a comfortable
seat, with some snacks, for I want a ringside seat...

Don't worry, the ~~Inquisitio SWILLus~~ -- the SWILL Inquisition -- has a nice comfy
seat waiting for you, ringside, but no snacks...

As the Wrath of the Trekkies rains down on your head! Trek has
had its time, and lots of it. It's been good and bad, and right
now with the so-called reboot, I think it could be much better
instead of loose remakes of old Trek movies. (There's a phrase
which proves I'm old...old Trek movies.) I want good stories, I
want a return to the original timeline, as original as it
gets with the modern series, like Voyager and the TNG movies.
Excellent exploration of the nearly 50 years of Trek, and it
definitely makes me want to ask, "And THEN what happened?" Space
opera, yes, but still there's some excellent adventures there.
Some TNG episodes are amazing even to this day. "Measure of a
Man", "The Inner Light"...some great stuff. I even liked the
way the DS9 cast was edited into the original tribble episode. Is
Trek too happyhappy? Perhaps, but it's a more pleasant
alternative to what leads the news these days.

Lloyd, you may be a Trekkie, but you are not a mindless Trekkie. There were some great episodes in the original series, as well as great episodes in TNG, less so in the later series in the franchise. Of the Star Trek films, I have said little (though Lester has spoken to this) because most of them suck shit, even the new ones. Almost all are rebooted/rehashed episodes from the television series' and overall, poor rehashes of these story ideas. Yes, it would be nice if someone could reboot the franchise (film or television) with some truly original material and story ideas; but, that is not going to happen -- they are going to go with what they consider to be safe and a proven money-maker.

As for the Wrath of the Trekkies, so far, not a peep. However, I will probably encounter some Trekkies at Ad Astra so I'm not out of the woods yet...

You may have to ease up on the trufen these days...they seem to be mostly in their 70s and 80s, and they are cranky, and they need their meds and their sleep. Trufandom, such as it is and was, seems to be on the way out. A shame in some ways, but in others, the dinosaurs did die out at some point. I think that's why Yvonne and I have been looking elsewhere within fandom, and finding other fun. Next month in Guelph is Genrecon, and we have a dealer's table up there, and Yvonne has agreed to be a masquerade judge. We may have some fun up there, who knows?

I have left the trufen alone since the Spring issue and that will continue until the 2014 Annual in February. There is not too much more to be said about these seniors of fandom... Of course, if any of them start sending in LoCs or commenting about how eevil it is that SWILL exists in other zines, then it is once again, open season.

How was Genrecon? How was it in comparison to ConBravo?

Gene Roddenberry was an LA police officer who, like many people in LA, decided to try his hand at screenwriting. He had a good

idea or two, but then, he imagined up Star Trek, and look what
happened there.

Yeah, he came up with a few good ideas, and Trek was one of them. I
am preaching to the choir here, sort of. You may be a Trek fan, but you
are not a real Trekkie from any of our discussions face-to-face or online.
I fully agree that Roddenberry had some good, perhaps even a couple of
great ideas, but he really was only, at best, a good producer. I believe
that we both agree that he had many failings and was neither a saint or
demigod as he is seen by many a Trekkie. However, I have never been
to your home, so for all I know you have a major shrine to Saint Gene in
your living room...

I'm getting mandatory re-education! Yay! University is far too
expensive these days! Neil and Lester are going to pay my way!
Thanks, guys! We did over $1000 business at Anime North, so are
we now capitalist reactionary bourgeoisie? Bring on the Trekkie
Inquisition. Now THEY certainly weren't expected.

Tsk-tsk... You display poor comprehension skills -- I did state that "you
must find your own transportation and pay all transportation costs"
Sorry to burst your bubble; besides, the fictional planet for Trekkie re-
education is reportedly, not a nice place. I cannot speak for the Trekkie
Inquisition, though I am definitely on their "list", but I can speak
regarding the SWILL Inquisition and you are currently on the list of
potential heretics...

Science fiction made my life easier because my own life as a
one-grade-ahead, smaller-than-everyone-else nerdy boy was rough.
No friends, and any activities I enjoyed were solitary. Off on a
bike ride by myself, for example. SF took me out of my humdrum
existence and took me to the Galactic Rim for adventures far
bigger than myself, and allowed me to meet impossible beings, and
lots of them. It satisfied the need for adventure in a dull time.
Fandom then brought all of us who felt that way together, and
perhaps gave us all friends for the first time in our lives. I
have friends from my initial days of fandom, which makes them
about 37 years in my acquaintance, and I can't think of any other

activity I could devote my time and life to that would get me that. One of those friends from my early days in Toronto fandom, I married.

As I mentioned last issue, discovering SF helped during the first few years in Ontario. In secondary school I was a nerd -- but of the "cooler?" weird nerd clique -- who had as our rivals the traditional nerd clique (the Math Club type). Us weird nerds made gunpowder in the chem lab and then blew up holes in the football field, we did other miscreant things as well (some of which if we did in secondary school today would result in a visit from CSIS or perhaps even USA Homeland Security), and our zenith (I think; Lester can rebut if I have this wrong) was the legal putsch of the Math Club (the holy of holy of our rivals) the rewriting of the club constitution, and disbanding of the club -- they would have to wait until next fall to re-form the club.

We've all enjoyed Star Trek together, and my earliest days in fandom included a brand new Star Trek club in Victoria, BC. Yet, even with the joy of those new friends, I still asked myself if there was more, and I did find the much larger world of SF fandom, and no regrets ever there. There was so much more to discover than in the world of Trek. I regret that I see so much of those early fannish days disappearing, although fandom itself carries on in a form many of my peers wouldn't recognize. I regret this, but I am not going to be the grumpy old man on the porch, snarling at the younger kids having fun on his front lawn. You've got to have your own fun, and in this case, we are by reinventing ourselves.

All I can say is the same thing I have said before to you and to Graeme. Fandom is changing and you don't necessarily have to change with it, but it may be more comfortable to change a bit. Otherwise, you become one of those "trufen" bitching about how this isn't the way we did things in 1979 and claiming that everyone outside of their group, the vast majority, is a fakefan. Or you can just do your own thing and ignore the changes. Or you can do your own thing and make some changes to fit in with the new fandom.

I still say this is a transition period. It will all work out in the end and there will still be fandom, in a modified form. The fact that the youth (under 30s) are organising their own fan-run conventions means that there will still be fan-run conventions and that type of fandom, its just that the style of programming will be a little different. I am not worried or concerned. Think about it; if we were to grab some forty year old fanzine fan from 1980 and bring them forward in time to attend Ad Astra 2015, they would initially claim that fandom has died and literary fandom has been overrun by the mediafen barbarians and that this, is, the end of days...

So yes, go ahead and reinvent yourselves within the changing fandom -- it's called adaptation ;)

Now that I've gone on at length, and much more length than I ever intended, I will shut this down, and say thanks. Our next convention is in October at Genrecon in Guelph, and we have a dealers' table there. In November will be SFContario 5, but we expect to be at the Toronto International Book Fest at the Metro Convention Centre a good portion of that weekend. Take it easy, our best to Lester, and see you next time. (I noticed, back to your regular name?)

A little more on that in the end part of the Endnote...

Yours, Lloyd Penney.

See you at Ad Astra -- I hope...

Endnote: The Starlost Singularity

Neil Jamieson-Williams

We begin this piece with the following announcement:

SWILL RETRACTION:

It is rare that SWILL makes a retraction -- never done in the Original SWILL -- but it does happen on occasion; it is more common in the current SWILL incarnation (as I am a middle-aged academic and not just a rabble-rouser in his 20s). And I am making this one so visible that even the most troglodytic of readers can not miss it, because this one is both important and germane to this issue's theme.

Over the years, and in SWILL (e.g. SWILL #14), I have recounted the tale of my very first SF convention, Fanfair 3 in Toronto in 1975. The central part of that story was my encounter with Harlan Ellison ® -- sort of. That encounter may indeed be apocryphal.

Here is a just-the-facts (based upon recall) of what happened. I would have arrived at the convention around 11:00 AM, Saturday August 2nd, 1975. I did not know anybody, I was sixteen years old, I had never been to a SF convention before, and I arrived wearing a Starlost t-shirt (one of our neighbours worked on the series). I don't know how long I was at the con before the incident happened, maybe about an hour. Two adults -- i.e. two men in their early to mid twenties grabbed me and then proceeded to carry me into the panel room -- one man had me by the shoulders and the other by my feet -- and presented me to the assembled panellists. One of the grown-ups (i.e. age 30 to 40) on the panel went ballistic over the t-shirt I was wearing screaming, "Get it out of here now, before I have it disembowelled." Laughing, the two men ran, still carrying me, from the panel room. Once outside set me down and one of them said, "We got Harlan Ellison." They then thanked me and walked away.

Now, being that I was a naive teenager from the burbs -- someone who had read Paingod and Other Delusions as well as Ellison stories in anthologies, who actually liked Ellison's stories, and who had no idea that Cordwainer Bird was one of Ellison's pen names -- I almost walked back into that panel room. However, some deep level of self preservation told me that I shouldn't, and that is exactly what I did.

In preparing for this issue of SWILL, I decided to dig into the past and see if I could find any supporting documentation to this tale. I couldn't find any. In part, there is very little in the way of documents. Waaay back forty years ago, small regional cons in Toronto didn't have very much actual information in their programme books -- for this panel, all that the programme book states is that there was one from Noon to 2 PM (no topic, no list of participants). In fact, the only actual evidence I have that the guy on the panel who went apeshit was Ellison, is that this is what the two young adults (who had temporarily abducted me) said that that person was, and from all appearances at the time -- the fact that they were congratulating themselves over the stunt -- they actually thought that that person was Ellison. Just some weak circumstantial evidence and nothing more...

Thus, I must state with all honesty, that the only evidence I have that the person on that panel was Ellison, is that the two fans in their twenties thought that that person was Ellison. Therefore, I retract the claim I have met Ellison twice - I only met him that one time at Westercon 37 (see this issue's Editorial).

RETRACTION ENDS:

Okay, so that is out of the way. As far as I can tell, I never, ever met Ellison at Fanfair 3 in 1975. I did have some unknown person go nutso over the Starlost t-shirt I was wearing that I was told was Ellison, but there is no evidence that that person was Harlan Ellison ®.

And so, we shall enter into the dangerous waters of Ellison and The Starlost (one more time), where your editor may -- at a later date -- be devoured by some Lovecraftian horror summoned forth by Ellison and/or his minions (or more probable, a letter by registered mail from Ellison's lawyer). Where the editor (wearing one of his other hats) of this pinnacle of literary perfection does find himself trapped within the event horizon of The Starlost and the litigious nature of Ellison. So, this attack has a personal aspect to it -- yes, it does involve my own enlightened self interest.

In SWILL #14 -- Starlost Memories -- I discuss The Starlost and state that, at the time that this series aired, that I liked it. I also state, in my defence, that I had just turned 14 and my previous experience with television SF was old Doctor Who serials and one single rerun of an original Star Trek episode.[9]   In brief, we didn't yet have cable and all of my experience with television was primarily Canadian television.

I have read Ellison's award winning teleplay "Phoenix Without Ashes", I have read the novel version by Ellison and Bryant, and the more recent graphic novel version. I have also read the shooting script of "Voyage of Discovery", production notes from CTV/Glen Warren, and I have interviewed two of the principal performers, and three of the F/X people over the years. And I have read other additional material over the past twenty odd years about, or alluding to, this series. The whole pre-production, production, and post-production of this project is akin to a fusion between American slapstick and a poorly written French farce and is a testimony to Murphy's Law. As I concluded in "Starlost Memories", this was a missed opportunity.

Yes, I agree with Ellison that "Phoenix Without Ashes" was superior to "Voyage of Discovery"; but it was not vastly superior, in my opinion (in contrast with the Star Trek episode "The City on the Edge of Forever" where Ellison's final script was indeed vastly superior to the shooting script for that episode). But, Klenman is also correct; "Phoenix Without Ashes" was (and still is) "biblical, heavy, and dull". In defence of the "heavy and dull", this is the first episode of the series -- it has to set the whole series universe up so there will be expository material that slows the pace. However, for someone who is not a member of the Abrahamic trio of faiths; yeah, the "biblical" charge stands.

How does "Phoenix Without Ashes" stand up today? It is good, but not wow! Yes, there are the interesting oppositions and subtexts for what was claimed to be a morality play for our times, but in

---

[9] We would spend a week at my uncle's cottage on Lake Memphremagog near the Quebec/Vermont border every summer and at night we could pull in a Vermont television station on the black and white television. The picture would be snowy, but watchable. In the summer of 1967, I watched the summer rerun of the episode "The Devil in the Dark". There was a thunderstorm outside and the picture was extra snowy and it scared me shitless. This was the only episode of Star Trek that I saw when the series was actually on the air -- however, I would watch the entire series years later when it was in syndication and when we also had cable.

reality is (as should be expected), a morality play of that time
-- the early 1970s. Yes, it has strong potential. But, it is
also flawed. One of the biggest flaws being the complete and
total lack of culture shock on the part of the character Devon (I
don't care how big a rebel and free thinker he is within the Neo-
Amish culture of Cypress Corners, he was nevertheless
enculturated/socialised within that restrictive culture; the
world outside his dome is going to unseat everything that he
knows, possibly even his own free-thinking heretic views) -- he
adjusts far too well. [10]

If anyone ever reboots this series, it will have to be heavily
updated. It would have to be made for a specialty channel as a
limited serial (the standard for European television drama) as
opposed to a broadcast television episodic series. And it would
have to -- and this is the hardest part -- receive the blessing
of Ellison. Which means, it isn't going to happen. After all,
Ellison threatens litigation over any story/film/television
programme/webseries that comes anywhere within a centimetre of
being remotely similar to The Starlost.

And here comes the rant... Ellison did not create the concept of
the generation starship as an interstellar "ark" -- that honour
goes to Tsiolkovsky and Bernal (and to a lesser extent to
Goddard). The trope that the inhabitants of a generation
starship will forget that they are on starship was first
introduced in the 1940s and 1950s. The concept that the
generation starship has gone off course (as well as the
inhabitants forgetting that they are on a ship) first appeared in
the 1960s. The only original concept that Ellison developed is
that the generation ship is composed of multiple biospheres and
multiple cultures (though Harrison sort of does this one -- with
two cultures -- in the late 1960s) and that it is on a collision
course with a star -- that's it, period. And yet, he behaves as
if all of the above are his original concept and potential
infringement of "Phoenix Without Ashes".

Well I have what was supposed to be a two novel series, sometimes
called a diptych, that examines the same far future culture using
two different modes of slower-than-light colonisation. Both
encounter hazards en route that creates the major plot device,
etc. In the first novel, they use a fleet of three colony ships
each with 20,000 colonists in stasis. In the second novel, they

---

[10] That said, this was written for episodic television of the 1970s -- you
only have 50 minutes to play with here.

use a world ship -- a huge habitat, made up of many valleys (each with a distinct culture) separated by mountains -- that is off course and on collision course with the target star. Based on the astrogation notes, provided by my friendly neighbourhood astrophysicist at the local university that I also lecture at, you do aim your starship for where the target star will be during acceleration mode, and the fine tuning of your trajectory -- so that you don't actually collide with the star -- would be performed after turn-around and during deceleration.

However, the second novel will not be written, nor is it in the works, beyond the world-building stage. Because, even though there is no Neo-Amish culture, nor is the world ship called an "ark", nor are they fleeing the destruction of the Earth, nor do the inhabitants not know that they are on a world ship -- even with all of that, I think crucial, difference, there is this old guy in Sherman Oaks, USA that, based on previous recorded behaviour, I am fairly certain, will go positively apeshit claiming that I am infringing on his copyright, his concept, his intellectual property, as he unleashes the lawyers. And because I have studied and written about The Starlost, I cannot claim that I wasn't inspired by, or influenced by this man's written work. Perhaps, after the swine croaks, I may be able to write this -- depending on how litigious his estate is -- and perhaps then someone may be able to reboot The Starlost and do it properly.

In the meantime, Mr. Ellison, here's the single finger salute!

The Name Game

After six years of being a thorn in their side, where I have managed to publish/present under alternative academic affiliation, under a different name, under my own imprint, and so on, my employer has decided to actually behave like a post-secondary institution of higher learning. I am now permitted to publish/present using my own name and proper academic affiliation so long as the work is scholarly. So, from here on in, there will be no use of Neil Williams or James William Neilson, just my legal name, Neil Jamieson-Williams (note: SWILL is not scholarly and I make no mention of my academic affiliation in SWILL).

Pith Helmet and Propeller Beanie Tour

April 2015 Ad Astra - Toronto (actually, the wilds of Markham...)

SWILL

science fiction
is the literature
of IDEAS

#26   Winter 2015

Table of Contents

SWILL is published quarterly (Spring, Summer, Autumn, and Winter) along with an annual every February - in other words, five times per year.

SWILL

Issue #26 Winter 2015

Copyright © 1981 - 2015 VileFen Press

a division of Klatha Entertainment an Uldune Media company

swill.uldunemedia.ca

Editorial: A Middle Class Phenomenon

Neil Jamieson-Williams

Lester didn't like the proposed sacred cow scheduled to be
slaughtered for this issue; so, we will go ahead with his instead
-- as it is, perhaps, a better sacred cow and a target that
permits me (at least) to sidebar onto my original along the way
(though not in this editorial). The norm that shall be
challenged in this issue is (for those who didn't look at the
front cover) the statement that "science fiction is a literature
of ideas".

This statement is one that has been used over the past half
century or so to defend the genre against the contempt it
receives from the literati and the high priesthood of the various
literary establishments. On the surface, the defence has its
merits; however, it is also a weak defence in that it is an
overgeneralisation and begs the question, which ideas? The best
work in our genre, may explore possibilities and push boundaries,
it may be radical or subversive -- holding up dominant social
paradigms and the current status quo for examination and critique
-- or philosophical, it may ask the questions "what if" of "if
this goes on", or it may place emphasis more on character and
plot. While science fiction may explore big ideas, dangerous
ideas drawn from either the natural sciences or the social
sciences (or better still, both), most of the time, our authors
are derelict in this duty -- and for good reason. Because, the
readership/viewership does not want it. They do not want to be
really challenged -- not at all. Oh, you can tweak their noses
here and there, but if you actually push the envelope, if you
challenge the normalised discourses of the genre on multiple
areas, the audience will deem the work to be too "mainstream",
"unrealistic", "difficult", etc. In other words, the kiss of
death for any writer of commercial fiction, which science fiction
is.

This is a subject that SWILL has touched on in the past, over the
years, and here we are at it again. Perhaps a little different
this time around. Malzberg said it best (my opinion):

"...science fiction is nothing -- anyone who ponders this for five minutes will see it clearly -- if it is not a middle-class phenomenon."[1]

And as science fiction IS a middle-class phenomenon, it will reflect the middle-class attitudes of the period it was written in. And the middle-class does not want to be challenged, period. Oh, they do want to be titillated, mildly jolted, maybe even have one or two of their buttons pushed, provided that they are also given some form of "techno-monkey" (see Lester's column) gosh-wow-sense-of-wonder. They are prepared to suspend disbelief so long as within that created science fictional world there is enough that remains familiar, i.e. most of it. No actual awesome jolts and never, ever, push all of their buttons. The readership, as a whole, will not stand for it, and will flee from the offending author (who better write a standard potboiler space opera for their next book to, partially, whitewash over the stain of failure for the sin of writing a novel that made a real attempt at cultural estrangement -- or face the stigma of now being unpublishable). Science fiction is a form of commercial literature. You can only get away with real cultural estrangement within the literary fiction genre and even then there are limits.[2]

One of the courses that I teach is Technology and Society and the General Education version of the course (taken as an elective) is usually filled with 40% Engineering/Computer Science students, 20% humanities students, 20% social science students, and 20% students for whom this is the only GenEd that fit in their timetables. The Engineering and CompSci students still tend to be the kids that would warm John W. Campbell's heart -- the eternal optimist "happy engineer" for whom technology is simply a problem solver and that any problems created by technology will be solved by more technology. The students from the Humanities usually tend to be of the "technology is evil" school of philosophy[3] and many of the social science students hold similar views and some of them are of the "technology is neutral" school.

---

[1] "Come Fool, Follify"; 1980 (Engines of the Night: 1982 or Breakfast in the Ruins: 2001)
[2] One limit is that those who write within this genre usually lack a science background and/or are unfamiliar with science fiction tropes (it is good to know what the rules are and what has been done before, before you go breaking and bending them) which reduces the power of their worldbuilding and extrapolation.
[3] Of course, this is usually a selective viewpoint; technology is never evil when it is providing smartphones, tablets, game consoles, etc.

Now, this is their views concerning our present, existing technologies. All of them are completely blown away by the latter part of the course when we examine emerging technologies and their potential impacts

For example, it is very plausible that within twenty years time every home will have a 3-D printer/microfacture device[4] that can build items, not just out of plastic, but out of other materials, including biological material. Say you decide that you want a new suit (and we are also going to make the assumption that this is not the first time you have purchased clothing this way, so that your household computing device(s) already have your 3-D scanned personal size data in its memory), you go online and find a design you like, purchase the design, and download it (if it is open-sources, just download it). Now, using your personal data, you have the software customise it to be a perfect fit, then send it to your 3-D printer/microfacture device, and voila, in a few hours you have a brand new, perfectly tailored, suit to wear. Cool, right? Definitely, gosh-wow; not as fast or as cool as a Star Trek replicator, but pretty much the same thing, though on a more limited scale. But how would this impact society?

Well, it would end retail as we know it. It would end manufacturing as we know it. And give a major shit-kicking to the transportation industry (what do you think is in most of those transport trucks on the highway?). And this will lead to large scale job losses in our society. And what are we going to do with all those big-box stores and all those manufacturing plants and so on? And what kind of economic domino-effect will this have? And this is just a minor extrapolation of greater capabilities for an existing consumer product that has a current price point that is the same as or less than the cost of a personal computer was twenty years ago.

My students usually are at first amazed at the prospect of having this consumer product at their command. But when confronted with the potential impacts of this new tech, they become uncertain and some are horrified and worried regarding their own future employment.

However, whatever the future will be, it will be different and science fiction will -- for the most part -- fail to predict that

---

[4] I use this term as this device as a consumer appliance would have to also have some limited robotic assembly features -- current 3-D printers are still for the at least the semi-skilled user and for anything more complicated than a fork, assembly is required.

future. And anyway, it is far more comfortable for science
fiction to illustrate a future where things are not too different
than today. Where today's middle-class sensibilities remain and
the middle-class sensibilities of the recent past are mocked and
critiqued. Where there is cheap interstellar travel, commodities
to be shipped near and far, and a human suburban sprawl in our
corner of the galaxy -- comfortable and middle class, of course
(unless you are one those the lower class people which we won't
discuss unless it is a "rags-to-riches" tale) -- and more a
pleasant wish-fulfilment fantasy than science fiction. And most
certainly, not a literature of ideas.

Thrashing Trufen: Cultural (Un)Estrangement

Neil Jamieson-Williams

Back in December Charles Stross posted the article *On the lack of cultural estrangement in SF* on his blog. Lester brought this to my attention and it is the central theme of this issue of SWILL. Science fiction as a literature of ideas, really does tend to fail, when it comes to cultural estrangement; Stross deftly illustrates this in his article that even a one century backward temporal shift within the same culture (UK) would throw up many issues of cultural estrangement for a person from the early 21st century. His other criticisms are equally valid regarding the genre.

While I do enjoy the work of Peter Hamilton, I know from the get-go that I will be reading "Essex suburbia goes interstellar" and just hope that the plot and/or characters are sufficient enough to carry the ride to its conclusion; I have never bailed on a Hamilton mega-novel (yet), but I have been disappointed. Hamilton is not alone in committing the sin of cultural unestrangement, both Stross and MacLeod are also sinners (but, to a far lesser degree) and they, at least, provide reasons why this is so. "So why do repeatedly we see the depiction of far future societies with cheap interstellar travel in which this hasn't bought about massive social change as a side-effect (other than the trivial example of everyone having a continental sized back yard to mow)?" Stross asks...

A very good question, indeed. Let's take it apart.

"Depictions of far future societies" is open to discussion, given the current pace of technological change. Usually this is placed at 500 years or more from the present, though some still set the beginning of "far future" at 10,000 CE (which is definitely far, but a little too far in my opinion). Barring a runaway Singularity, I would hypothesise that the near future begins with tomorrow and ends roughly 150 years from now, messo future overlaps this beginning as early as 100 years from present to about 300 years from present, and far future overlaid again, beginning perhaps as early as 200 years from present. The big questions here being, will there be some form of technological singularity, and if there isn't, will there be some form of technological plateau, or slow down.

Contrary to the boosterism of the technological optimists, if a technological singularity is not reached within the next two centuries, that means that the emerging technologies of bioengineering, nanotechnology, and artificial intelligence (in whole or in part) will actually be more difficult to develop to maturity than the optimists currently predict. That will also mean that the exponential rate of technological advancement will stall or slow down rapidly. This has happened before, usually for cultural reasons -- that we have cultural blinders on, from our worldview, that prevent us from imagining a particular breakthrough, or from perceiving the utility of a specific technology, or our model of the universe is in error and we have yet to see that there is an error. However, even if our rate of technological advancement slows or stalls over the next two hundred years, we are still going to have some very powerful technologies available -- all of them being game-changers.

Bottom-line, even if the exponential rate of technological change grinds to a halt; societies, even a mere two hundred years from now are going to be strange from our early 21st century point of view. If 1915 is a sort of familiar yet alien world to a person from 2015; 2215 will probably be even more alien and less familiar. To continue with just one technology (the same one used in the Editorial 3D printing/microfacture) this technology is going to change everything and is being developed faster than initially expected.[5] However, its impact, even over the next 50 years, is going to be overwhelming. There is no way our current economic system can survive this technology without massive structural reforms[6] or a decent into corporate tyranny (and the latter is unsustainable).[7] What roads are taken will depend upon

_____

[5] *Synthesis of many different types of organic small molecules using one automated process* Science 13 March 2015
[6] When Lenin said, "The Capitalists will sell us the rope with which we will hang them."; he may have been right, just not in the literal sense that he was speaking in. Industrial capitalism, in developing and implementing and marketing and advancing 3D printing -- all in the name of reducing labour and overhead -- may indeed have manufactured and sold the figurative rope that will terminate this economic system (at least as we currently know it).
[7] Yes, our current elites are strongly in favour of returning to their version of the "good old days", when the vast mass of ordinary people lived in poverty and deprivation (1915 is close enough, though they would like to turn the clock back to the 1870s) with little political power and a small wealthy elite ruled almost unopposed. This worked a century or so ago because the elite

individual nation states and their government-of-the-day, but
within the nation-states that are democracies (or where the
citizens still, at least, believe that they live in a democracy),
it is more probable that massive reforms will occur. 3D printing
will be a major job-killer and lead to massive adult unemployment
and massive adult unemployment becomes a government problem and
governments don't like the types of problems that can lead to
civil unrest/revolution and democratic (real or facade)
governments will tend to choose to make reforms (even if it
angers those who donated to their election campaigns) rather that
use state violence to quell real or potential unrest. Of course,
this all depends upon the attitudes of the current leader and the
party in power -- if this was a current problem here in Canada,
our current Prime Minister and his party would opt for state
violence over systemic reforms. Thing is, if this technology
continues to develop at its current rate and reach maturity over
the next thirty years (which it shows all probability of doing),
2075 may be as alien to a person from 2015 as is 1915. And this
is only looking at a single technology.

One that that we can be very certain of, a society 200 years from
the present, is going to have very little in common with a neo-
liberal capitalist, suburban society of 2015. In all
probability, a society in 2215 (if our technological civilisation
does survive -- we could still crash the whole thing) will be a
post-scarcity economy (maybe libertarian, maybe anarchist, maybe
socialist, maybe all of the above) and residence patterns will
vary between the culture(s) of each society and their individuals
-- it will be a mix, a melange between urban and rural with very
little suburban (the whole point of suburban being that you
cannot afford to live in the urban centre, but do have to go
there to work). As for 500 years or 1,000 years from the present
-- it now starts to become highly improbable that there would be
any society that is like a neo-liberal capitalist, suburban,
representative democratic society of the early 21st century,
period.

---

still needed ordinary people to work the machines, etc. to produce the goods
and services that made the elite wealthy. But, with advanced 3D printing, our
labour is no longer needed. If the technology produces 40% to 60% adult
unemployment, who is going to buy the goods and services to continue to keep
the elite wealthy? And what are governments going to do with all the
unemployed? And then there are the conspiracy theorists (both on the right
and the left) who claim that the elite plan is to reduce the surplus
population -- i.e. exterminate the majority of citizens -- to restore a
balance (a kind of terminal market correction).

So far, I have just discussed potential societal changes over the next 200 years (usually not far future territory). What about space?

Space is hostile, space is hard. Even with mature 3D printing/microfacture, even with fully mature bioengineering, nanotechnology, and artificial intelligence (sans runaway), interplanetary space travel and colonisation is going to be difficult -- doable and feasible -- but difficult. Will it ever be cheap? That would all depend upon drive capabilities. If the fuel is inexpensive and the velocities sufficient, it is conceivable that we could achieve drives that allow for travel from Earth to Mars (average distance) one-way within 9 days to a fortnight, which would place the entire solar system in our grasp as a species.

As for "cheap interstellar travel", that would require FTL that is inexpensive and does not necessitate mega-engineering on the scale of a near Type II civilisation. Thus, what we think we know about physics would have to be horribly incomplete or in error, for us to still have an, essentially, Type I civilisation capable of flitting about the galaxy at superluminal velocities. And, even then, nobody is going to bother with shipping Lemto cheese from one star to another -- they would just microfacture it at home. At the end of the day, even with current physics being wrong (thus permitting inexpensive, rapid, "magic box" FTL sans mega-engineering), even with our civilisation(s) remaining at a Type I level, even if we fudge things so that bioengineering/nanotechnology/artificial intelligence do not fully mature (just develop enough to make our lives more comfortable), this future interstellar civilisation is not going to be anything like an early 21st century society. Not one bit...

And so we stack the deck, descend into wish-fulfilment, etc. so that these societies ARE like an early 21st century society -- otherwise the editors and the readership would flee these shores for safer harbours within the genre. While fans, and editors, and critics, and writers may pay lip service to the genre being a literature of ideas (i.e. that this is part of our ideal culture); this is little more than an invocation or supplication in SF's real culture.

Pissing on a Pile of Old Amazings

A mXModest Column by Lester Rainsford

Recently a $BigNameProAuthor
reXeXcXcXoXoXuXuXnXnXtXtXeXeXXddX complained that he'd
stopped reading an 1100 page book 50 pAges before the end.
The problem? Lack of 'culturla estrangement'. Translated
from BigNameProQuthorese, this means, thousands of years
into an interstellar future, it's the society of today. And
for the BNPA that simply wasn't enough to hold his attention
to the bitter end.

The claims of "SF is a literature of IDEAS!!" need to
explain how this can be. Where are the ideas? Well, the
ideas must be somewhere else, other than the society and the
characters in the story. Maybe in the neat tech? To Lester,
this kind of defence is going back to the Gernsback days,
where a story idea could be, say, "what if we could develop
a triode with intrinsic superheterodyining?" To certain
obsessed geeks a triod with intrinsic superheterhodyning is
the cat's meow, but it's the sort of idea that's better
fXoXrXXXa as a basis for an article in Home Radio Hobbyist
than a basis for an 1100 page sci-fi epic.

Oddly, in the discussion that ensued over the BNPA's
declaration, Lester did not see anyone posit that tX one
glaring answer was right in the setup. A couple of other
answers glare at Lester, and those are that: i) it's not
1954 anymore; and ii) it's still not 1954 anymore.

If Lester grants that the author of the 1100 page book has
some intelligence, skills, and craft, the pXrXoXbXlXeXmX
answer to the problem, or at least one of them, is apparent.
It's hard work thinking up a radically different future
society, it's hard work thinking up how people will behave
and interact, and it's impossible to get it right anyway.X--
at least over the spread of 1100 pages. Even a skilled
author will slip up, put in anachronisms, and will miss
things that any number of alert readers will catch. Plus, it
simply does not pay to think up an extremely detailed 4000-
years-in-the-future society, and work out why everything is

the way it is, and then write a story in that background. It doesn't pay because it would take years, perhaps several lifetimes, and during those liftemes thechnological change today will make certain of your assumptions about 6015AD ob solete, and you will get to start all over again. Ugh. So authors, who after all are trying to make a living at this kind of thing, cut corners. Take a vaguely modern society, trap it up with Cool Tech drapes, and assume that your "look! a mohkey!" misdirection holds readers' attention. The vaguely modern society makes it easier for both the author (because it's their default environment, it's easy to write about and comes naturally) and the reader (who is not puzzling out how an utterly unfamiliar society works and can possibly work). A placid SF reader isn't going to think; and in not thinking, the placid SF reader won't spot worldbuilding flaws and ask awkward questiosn about them.

Lester is a slow reader, and this makes him prone to thinking about the background and plot. This is rXaXrXeXlXyX never propitionus to the enjoyment of the work. Complain, complain, complain--that's Lester's lot in SF reading life.

Anotgher problem with the cultural background is that it's not 1954 anymore. Back in 1954, a huge swath of the SF authors had participated in World War II. This means they got sent to faraway places on short notice to do what they could in the war effort. In a few years, someone living on a farm that lacked electricity might be flying a state-of-the-art multiengine bomber with pressurixation and remote-controlled gun turrets. How's _that_ for cultural estrangement? Okay, maybe that's still Gernsbackian, but one way or another they also got to interact with different cultures, some of which may have been quite isolated before their territory became a key stragegic asset. So after the war, these authors had some familiarity with diverse cultures and countries, and they could put it into their writing. OXkXaXyX,XXXsXoXXWhen Jack Vance (who was in the merchant marine if Lester recalls correctly) puts a story on "Yap", maybe it really is the Yap that actually exists in the South Pacific. But, to the reader, at least the culture of a small island in the South Pacific is going to be a heck

of a lot less familiar than the culture of their home town
and friends and neighbours. So, cultural estranment is
achieved.

Another problem with it not being 1954 anymore is that there
are hardly any SF magazines these days, and the magazine
market is barely more than a pimple iXnX on the body of
annual SF publication, and that means that the short story
is irrelevant today, except amongst the cognoscenti. Lester
doesn't <u>want</u> to be part of the cognoscenti, but some days he
feels there's little choice.

In a 3000 word short story or a 10,000 word novella, the
author can put in a new idea, have a bit of fun with it, and
be done. There is no need to come up with the enormous
background information that's needed for an 1100 page novel,
nor any need to worry, over each of those 1100 pages, that
there's something inconsistent, either with the supposed
future, or with the supposed future itself.

So, Lester's take on "why can't an 1100 page SF novel have
cultural estrangement" is, <u>are you kidding</u>? Damn thing's
impossible. Frank Herb ert may have come close with <u>Dune</u> and
CXhXiXlXDune Messiah, but how many times in SF has this feat
been managed? Not very often! Not that Dune and Dune
Messiah, both together, come anywhere close to 1100 pages.
(Lester dXaXyXsX,Xsays, read those two, then stop. Your life
will be better that way.) It's obvious that the 1100 page
novel will have lots of padding, lots of overextended
descriptions in ever-fractalling detail, and precious little
in the way of a different society.

Lester guesses that the majority of today's SF writers make
their living, one way or another, sitting in front of a
keyboard staring at a computer screen. Of course the pro
author is doing so in creation of their work, but for those
who are not full-time, their "XrXeXaX1X"day" job is likely
staring at the computer as well. So that's the kind of
society and future they can imagine, and certainly that's
the kind of society and future they find easiest, most
natural, to write about. Gone are the days of being posted

to some obscure part of the world on some obscure mission
that no one seems to know the details about. (For all the
wXaXbXnXkXiXnXgX wanking about the Cloud and Big Data, World
War II ran on paper and filing cabinets and carbon paper
inserted in typewriters.)

Of course a superheterodying triode is not enough techno-
dressing to cloak an 1100 page novel with "literature of
IDEAS" garb. But, throw in "food in a pill!" and "space will
be AwesomeExcellent once pesky NASA gets out of the way!"
and also "of course relativity is bunk",throw in a gadget or
two (try not to be too obvious in ripping off Sapple/Samsung
new product developments for the next year), and there you
go. Look! A monkey! An IKEA monkey! (It's all ideas!)

To add insult to the injuries inflicted on Lester, when
authors start playing with "let's make the culture strange",
this all to often is code for "I got my ideas and fixation,
and the world would run a goldarned lot better if it worked
the way I would prefer it, so my new novel will feature the
wonderful world where my kinks are perfectly respectable and
accepted aXnXdX nay desired by all!"

That is Heinlein in a nutshell. Particularly late Heinlein,
but it was there right in his earliestmX, previously
unpublished work For Us the Living. Of course Heinlein is
far from the only pinata that can be beaten with this
particular stick--Lester is, for examply, not particularly
fond of Delany's obvious fascination with cracked knuckles
and thick fingernails. Again, that's obvious in Delany's
later work, but hints show up in the good earlier stuff,
such as Nova.

As long as readers fall for "look! a technomonkey!" tricks,
and demand 1100 page novels (fourth bXoXoXkX volume of the
googoplexian epic!), SF won't be a literature of ideas. It
simply can't be. If it wants to be, it needs to change.
Somehow, Lester figures that the interests of authors to be
published and to be paid will overbalance the need to
justify, with concrete examples, that SF is a "literature
of ideas".

Flogging a Dead Trekkie:

Violating the ~~Taboos~~ Norms of Science Fiction

Part 9 of 8 – Three Extra Taboos

Neil Jamieson-Williams

Ah, I forgot that in "Thus Our Words Unspoken" in the second half of Breakfast in the Ruins (the material written in the early 2000s) Malzberg introduces three additional Taboos of Science Fiction. And, in the case of this trio, the word taboo is applicable over norm violation. All three are strongly linked to biology and raise the hotly debated questions of Nature vs. Nurture in regards to cultural traits and individual and collective behaviour. All three ask us to look at traits, usually seen as repugnant within Western industrial societies (though not perhaps for those who are members of the Conservative Party or USA Republicans), in a positive light -- i.e. that from an evolutionary perspective, they have survival value.

The three additional taboos are: XENOPHOBIA as a species survival mechanism, BIOLOGICAL IMPERATIVE aka "Biology is destiny", and RAPE AS THE PERPETUATION OF BIOLOGICAL CHARACTERISTICS WHICH COULD NOT OTHERWISE CARRY FORTH. Pretty, eh?

Let's deal with the most repugnant first, NORM VIOLATION TEN (aka TABOO 3: this is indeed the reproductive strategy for the dominant males in a chimpanzee troop; male initiated gendered aggression is common among chimps. While there have been some studies that do indicate that sub-dominant males in a chimpanzee troop do use rape as a reproductive strategy, sub-dominant males more often employ bribery and stealth as method of containing their genetic line (they bribe a female in oestrus, with food, to follow them into the bush away from the group). Any claim that this is how our pre-human ancestors behaved, has to be questioned. Just because chimpanzees behave this way, doesn't lead to the conclusion that the last common ancestor between humans and chimps possessed this behaviour. After all, bonobos don't; instead they use consential sex as conflict resolution. The split in the chimp/bonobo line occurred roughly 1.5 million years ago and the human/ancestral chimp line diverged messily (diverging, then hybridisation, then a final split) between 7 and 5 million years ago. The ancestral chimp (precursor to both the chimpanzee and the bonobo) could easily have had a behavioural pattern closer to that of the bonobo than what is seen in the contemporary chimpanzee. It is quite probable that the more aggressive behaviour of the chimpanzee came after the divergence 1.5 million years ago.

The same can be said regarding NORM VIOLATION EIGHT (aka TABOO 1). While the chimpanzee does engage in xenophobic behaviour, bonobos do not. Humans fit, somewhere in the middle and, at our worst, we do exhibit chimpanzee level xenophobia made more destructive by our technology. At our worst, that is; keep in mind that the majority of the human population does not consider people like Thomas of Torquemada, Oliver Cromwell, Talaat Pasha, Adolph Hitler, Joseph Stalin, Mao Zedong, Pol Pot, Augustin Bizimungu, etc. to be exemplars -- they are aberrations. They would be chimpanzee exemplars, though. If we were as xenophobic as the chimpanzee, we would not have survived the 20th century. (even without nuclear weapons) there would have been a H. G. Wells type of total and endless war with 1920s technology fought to the bitter end of societal collapse worldwide -- with nuclear weapons, probable extinction. We are more co-operative than the chimpanzee and not as co-operative as the bonobo; we are less aggressive than the chimpanzee and more aggressive than the bonobo; we are less xenophobic than the chimpanzee and more xenophobic than the bonobo. And, we are more intelligent than both the bonobo and the chimpanzee.

Is xenophobia a survival trait? I don't know. It has been selected in the past; after all, it is not a trait that is necessarily maladaptive[8] so long as you are hunter-gatherers or

---

[8] Note: often a culture's name for themselves within their own language translates as "the people" or "the human beings" meaning that "others" are not...

small scale horticulturalists, or pastoral herders. That is until your society starts to get big, about 5,000 people or more -- then it can be problematic. Once you move to intensive agriculture, and the dawn of civilisation and empire and cosmopolitan living, xenophobia may be handy for your warriors, but you certainly don't want that trait within the general population, certainly not among your peasants. In fact, we have being domesticating ourselves over the past 7,000 years (or at least the past 5,000 years) as our local population sizes increased -- we weren't doing this intentionally, but we were doing it nevertheless. Because we have xenophobic traits, this is why it is a common trope within SF that we use this trait to unite humankind against the alien menace -- you are just expanding the membership from tribe/nation-state to species. If the cosmos is a nasty, nihilistic social environment -- if people like the late Carl Sagan are horribly wrong about the behaviour of other intelligent species[9], then xenophobia (a moderate amount) may indeed be a survival trait.

NORM VIOLATION NINE (aka TABOO 2)-- the old Freud statement that biology is destiny is at the root, the centre, of each of these three violations/taboos in a nutshell. How much of our behaviour is written in our biology and how much is learned behaviour. We do not know all the answers here. While biology is indeed important, it is not the sole determiner of destiny. Environment plays a critical factor regarding epigenetics and for species like ourselves, culture also plays a major role in our destiny. The biological imperative or biological determinism is, at present, a less strong of an argument than it was fifteen years

---

[9] That other intelligent species would be non-hostile, wise guides for newer intelligences. Some may indeed be; but, not all. Neither would they all be the uber-rapacious species that want to strip our biosphere, or process us as food, or occupy our planet, though some species may be like that. But, those species would be viewed as pests by older, more powerful, species -- pests that must be contained or, if necessary, eradicated. Or maybe what is common is something in-between: it's like an American "wild west" out there, where almost anything goes, so long as you don't piss off/attract the interest of the transcendent AIs or whatever form the "ancient ones" take. That means that "savages" such as ourselves would be fair game to be exploited by species that are just a few centuries or so more technologically advanced than us. In short, other species may be nasty and xenophobic and there may be no galactic federation to protect our rights...

ago. Yes, biology is important, but biology isn't everything --
at least not yet.

We have been engaged in a human domestication programme for
several thousand years, most of the time unintentionally and
unknowingly. Across the span of millennia, only recently -- the
past 150 years -- have we begun to understand the mechanisms
involved, so our direction has been erratic. Up until now, there
was still some level of randomness, some degree of natural
selection being employed (though increasingly modified and
mitigated by culture). That could all change in the near future.
Once we figure out how to work epigenetics and genetics at will -
- human guided biology will be destiny. The big question though;
who will be at the controls?

Scribbling on the Bog Wall

Letters of Comment

Neil Jamieson-Williams

As I write this, there is one LoC from the usual suspect (Lloyd) and two reviews. My comments are, of course, in glorious pudmonkey.

1706-24 Eva Rd.
Etobicoke, ON
M9C 2B2

January 14, 2015

Dear Neil:

Sorry it's taken a while.thanks for issue 25 of Swill, and congrats on 25 issues! I see to celebrate, you are taking on SF's most vicious target. Good luck on this one.

As it turns out, no sound and no fury, not even a whimper...

Harlan was once an Angry Young Man, but has become an Angry Old Fart. Yet, he recently shook off a stroke like it was a head cold, so maybe he really is a force of nature. And whatever you might say about him, should he find out, I wouldn't put coming up here to find you past him. (And as I read on, I see you agree with me. Don't poke the crankyman with a stick.) Don't hit him with anything about the Last Dangerous Visions.that little gem is close to 40 years old, I think, and some of his contributors have died waiting for him to get on with it. Has no one dared to smack this old man, even when he was younger? A sound thrashing/ass-kicking might have changed him for the better.

Hey, this is SWILL. We will poke the crankyman with a stick, regardless of all warnings. I will face the music, should it come to that. His Angry Old Fartness rarely visits the Great White North and probably would consider it beneath him to respond to SWILL in any manner (other than a lawsuit). I retract nothing from SWILL #25. Bring it on Harlie-boy...

I have read SF written by feminists, and it can be very good, with some clear messages. I am told to listen to their messages, and I try, but often the messages relayed by different groups are confused to the point of being contradictory. That says to me that both genders are confused as to the best way to sexual equality.

I think that feminist SF is still a work in progress, i.e. it is still evolving. While I do support there being a feminist SF; as a reader, I am neutral. I have disliked more works of feminist SF that I have read than there being works that I have liked and enjoyed. I tend to be frugal when this happens and I am more willing to try feminist SF short fiction than make the investment regarding novel-length works.

I'm still the only one to respond to this zine? How many readers do you have, anyway? I hope more than just me. Genrecon vs. ConBravo? Genrecon reminded me and Yvonne of old Ad Astras from years past. We had a great time, and we made some money, too. ConBravo, we were there to see what it was like. not much in the way of programming, but one gigantic dealers' room. As a potential vendor for this year, I've got to say good, and there's opportunity for a profitable weekend. I hope to get to both conventions in 2015.

ConBravo was nothing more than a dealers room and, for the admission price, not worth the effort. For this type of tradeshow con, I'd rather trek down to Toronto for Fan Expo.

The newer fandoms I have become involved with are steampunk, which doesn't take it self seriously, which is part of the fun, and the fandom surrounding the CBC show Murdoch Mysteries.we've been on the ground floor for this, and we see the same things happening in it as happened in SF fandom.lots of friends made, organizations, get-togethers and major events, and yes, even the obsessed fan that makes the production company wonder about the whole lot of us. Adaptation it is, and we're still sticking around to see how it all boils down.

Shrug. Steampunk, sort of interesting, but not actually my thing... I know that you both really are strong fans of Murdoch Mysteries -- I am not, and we will leave it at that.

Yes, we will be at Ad Astra, and we have taken a dealer's table, to see if we can sell some more steampunk and neoVictorian jewelry, sit on our butts all weekend, and enjoy a leisure-filled weekend. We will see you there. Let me know when the next issue is planned, and I can be a little better prepared for its arrival.

Yours, Lloyd Penney.

See you at Ad Astra...

Amazing Stories
The Clubhouse: Fanzine Reviews: Into the Abyss.
R. Graeme Cameron
January 2, 2015

SWILL (#25) - Autumn 2014 - Find it here

Faned: Neil Williams. Canadian Perzine.

This is very much a Curmudgeon zine in that it is written by perhaps the most iconoclastic fan in zinedom. Poor lad can't help it, what with carrying on a tradition he first established in the 1980s and has now renewed with his reborn SWILL.

Let me quote from his editorial (though bear in mind he is temporising here): "In March 26th, 2014 I decided that in keeping with the unannounced theme-arc of SWILL 2014 - that of norm violation and attacking sacred cows - that the Autumn issue would be an anti-Ellison issue. On October 10, 2014, Harlan Ellison ® suffered a stroke, which was announced in the media on October 12th. Even I, the evil anti-fan editor, did consider changing the planned autumn 'trash Ellison' issue, due to his illness. However, as the updates continue to come in, it would appear that Ellison is recovering well, that his mind has been unaffected, and that his physiotherapy is making progress - and, he is already writing again. As this is the situation, and, after all, as this is SWILL, there is no longer any concern, on my part, that I am kicking-someone-when-they-are-already-down. This is not as mean spirited as it sounds…"

Neil goes on to admit he admires much of Ellison's writings, but finds Harlan's attitude toward fans, indeed, entire generations of fans, to be reprehensible and without merit. Coming from someone who is "anti-fan" himself, this is interesting. I would say Neil considers Ellison to be "too much" of a curmudgeon.

No Graeme, you got me wrong here. Yes, I do admire Ellison's works. But, I also admire Ellison's attitude toward fandom -- definitely a sort of "kindred spirit", so to speak. I take exception to Ellison's general misanthropy, that he doesn't always practice what he preaches, has an

American-centric worldview, and does not always behave well in public...

Frequent guest editorialist Lester Rainsford (the title of his regular column is "Pissing on an Old Pile of Amazings") carries on the theme, writing:

"Do you know that there is one person in the world who ever got ripped off by other people?... one person with the guts and the clear-headed orneriness to declare that he got ripped off and oppressed by the Man right in public?... one person in the whole entire world who has held on to Artistic Integrity when all the luddite know-nothing philistines have sold out to mammon and convenience?... and moreover has declared that he has been hard done by, and deserves the greatest of praise and respect thereby, to right the wrongs done to him?"

Yes, Lester's modest column is so underappreciated."

But to hear Harlan Ellison talk about this, he is even worse done by."

Neil and Lester and Harlan at their best (or worst?) are kindred spirits. Certainly none of them pull any punches. Not ever.

The letter of comment column has but one participant. You guessed it. Lloyd Penney.

Swill worth reading? - Hell, yes! If, that is, like me, you find over-the-top editorializing exhilarating and exciting. That's why I like Ellison in full fury. Even when he's wrong he's vastly entertaining and guaranteed to shake you out of your doldrums. Neil and Lester likewise.

On the other hand, SWILL is definitely an acquired taste and not for everyone. If you have high blood pressure reading SWILL could give you apoplexy. So beware.

One thing's for sure. Never a dull issue. Not one.

Graeme, thank you for your review and understanding (Lester, in particular, thanks you for noticing how unappreciated he is). What I always like about your commentary is that you actually get the concept of SWILL. And yes, SWILL is most definitely an acquired taste, one that did not seem to sit too well on the palette of our next reviewer...

The zine dump
No. 33
A zine about zines
by Guy h. Lillian III

Swill #25 / Neil Jamieson-Williams, swill.uldunemedia.ca / The issue dates to
last August, but only today blossomed in my e-mailbox.

Somewhat confused here, comrade... I did send you an email back in
May with a link to SWILL #23 plus a link to our back issues. I also sent
you a link to SWILL #24 in September. And in mid December I sent
you an email with the link to SWILL #25; regardless, you did review
SWILL #25 -- thanks.

Devoted to "norm violation and attacking sacred cows," according to the
editor, this is an "anti-Ellison," as in Harlan Ellison, issue, with further
pieces on "Trashing Trufen", "Flogging a Dead Trekkie", and "Pissing on a Pile
of Old Amazings". Considering the mild flavor of this issue's fanzines, with
little in the way of controversy, this should make Swill (founded 1981, it
says here) a welcome diversion. Certainly the antique and purposefully blotty
typewriter fonts convey a rebellious, defiantly trashy attitude.

SWILL in its current incarnation normally has the following
features/columns: Editorial, Thrashing Trufen, Pissing on a Pile of Old
Amazings, Flogging a Dead Trekkie, Scribbling on the Bog Wall, and
Endnote -- each of which, with the exceptions of Pissing on a Pile of Old
Amazings and Scribbling on the Bog Wall, have a unique subtitle each
issue. SWILL was founded in 1981, see the back issues, Original
SWILL.

Anyway, after an acknowledgment of Harlan's recent poor health and insistence
that his recovery makes him again, fair game, Jamieson-Williams does indeed go
after him. Despite admiring much of his writing, Neil calls Ellison a
misanthrope who thinks all human beings are scum, a "yellow journalist" for
not checking his sources adequately, and finally an "arsehole," just on
general principles.

Yes, I did do all of that. I take full responsibility and make no
apologies...

Moving on to trufen, Neil's article is mostly more Harlan; a sharper jab comes
in the lettercol from Lloyd Penney: "You may have to ease up on the trufen
these days ... they seem to be mostly in their 70s and 80s, and they are
cranky, and they need their meds and their sleep."

Unclear as to whether you are discussing Trashing Trufen (the subtitle of the piece this issue is An Archetypical Anti-Fan and is actually more in praise of Ellison than against him) or Scribbling on the Bog Wall (the lettercol).

Amidst the strikeouts, contributor Lester Rainsford is supposed to pee on Amazing, but also tries to trash Harlan. I can't figure out what this has to do with Amazing.

Ah, you neither understand the context or the mystery... I cannot explain the mystery as even I do not know the true reason why Lester chose this as the title of his column. I can explain the context, Pissing on a Pile of Old Amazings, has been the title of Lester's column since SWILL #1 in 1981.

Again taking up the typewriter, Neil ponders genuine feminist SF, admitting that he doesn't know what that means. I feel his pain; I don't know what Swill means. Says Neil, "Swill has always been very adept at prodding at soft spots and pushing buttons in the past." Balloon-poppers in an oft-pompous venue such as fandom are always welcome, but effective iconoclasty needs specifics to back up the button-punching, and here I mostly see nastiness for its own sake. Well, try me again.

Ah, well SWILL has often been accused over the years of being nasty or mean just for the sake of being mean and nasty. We do not deny this -- it is part of the spirit of SWILL -- though we also believe that we offer valid criticism along with the mean and nasty iconoclasm. Do try SWILL again, or even look over some of the back issues...

[I'm prejudiced here; I genuinely admire Harlan Ellison and miss those days of The Glass Teat and Dangerous Visions (though I yearn for the final volume too) when he was the hope of the field. As for his personality, well, he gave me a boost when I was a kid that I have neither forgotten nor fulfilled, and I number him with Alfred Bester, Julie Schwartz, Fred Chappell, Lillian Hellman, and a zillion people no one's ever heard of as mentors to whom I owe an unpayable debt.]

I am probably more in agreement with you than you think. SWILL has often praised Ellison and defended his position on certain issues. It was deemed time to also take some pokes at him, as he is indeed fallible. As stated in the issue, the concept of an Anti-Ellison issue was conceived back in March 2014 and publication of the Autumn issue was delayed almost two months, just to make certain that he was actually recovering.

Endnote: The KD[10] of Literature

Neil Jamieson-Williams

Science fiction could be a literature of ideas, but most of the time it is not, period. Some of the time, an attempt is made, and more often than not, the attempt fails. It may fail in that it is preachy -- this is the way the author thinks that the world should be like -- or, less often, it is too strange, but not literary enough, and thus never finds an audience. And some of the time, the attempt is successful, only to be swept into the trashbin by the passage of time and rapid technological change -- it becomes dated. Most of the time, though; the goal is not even attempted.

I have discussed this before in issues past (and in previous incarnations of SWILL), both Lester and I have touched on it this issue. And I will now say it again. A true "literature of ideas" science fiction novel would have the average SF fan running for cover. It would not find a publisher (not as big a problem today with self-publishing) and would have difficulty finding an audience. It would have to have enough literary elements within it to spark any interest among the literati (who would accept the strangeness of a true SF world provide that the conventions of their genre were also met). There may be some SDF reader who would read the book and enjoy it, most would hate it and post their venomous screeds (in a SWILL-like fashion) all over the internet and in particular at Amazon, ChaptersIndigo, and Kobo.

Professional writers, those who do this for a living, really like to get paid for their work -- this is their job, their source of income -- and are not usually going to write career-killing novels (or this is a mistake they make once, and then never again) or demand that their publisher publish this far future novel that is virtually incomprehensible to the average reader (because no publisher is going to intentionally publish something that they know they are going to lose money on -- publishers like to receive paycheques too). Oh, yes; you can shout out, where is

---

[10] For Americans and other foreigners; Kraft brand macaroni and cheese is marketed as Kraft Dinner in Canada and for Canadians, all macaroni and cheese that comes in a box that you make yourself is called Kraft Dinner, or KD for short.

the art? Have you no ethics? Have you no integrity? But, face
it; part of being an adult is that you learn to choose your
battles and to know when to fight and when to retreat.'' And
guess what; even I do not want to read a steady diet of
difficult, weird, truly alien human cultural setting novels.
Maybe one or two a year, and that's it -- and thank the gods for
self-publishing because it can allow our professional writers to
experiment, should they choose to do so, now and again.

I read more than SF, I do read some political thrillers and
mysteries, and I do read mainstream (actually the current novel I
am reading is mainstream Canadian fiction); but most of what I
read is SF. I like the juxtaposition that SF presents, it may
just be one of Lester's "techno-monkeys" or it may have greater
substance, whatever, it sparks my interest. A good writer will,
most of the time, be able to carry me along right to the
conclusion. But, in the end, most SF is literary comfort food;
most SF is the KD of literature.

Pith Helmet and Propeller Beanie Tour

April 2015 Ad Astra - Toronto (actually, the wilds of Markham…)

'' I learned this working in radio -- a collaborative medium -- on a sub-
miniscule budgets (which allowed for a greater degree of writer creative
control, because there wasn't a lot of money involved, but unlike the prose
writer, you really do have to work, and be able to work harmoniously, with
other people to get the final series/show made). My forays into film never
really amounted to much, other than money -- everybody knows this now, but
just in case you are one of the few who don't -- the media conglomerates buy
(don't know the current ratio) way more scripts than they ever produce into a
movie. Only five of my scripts ever got the green light and only one made it
into principal photography (by which time, it had been so heavily re-written
that I no longer had a credit on it (the original script was a drama and the
shooting script was a teen comedy) and it went direct to video and I am not
going to name it (to protect both the innocent and the guilty) and, anyway,
all that was left from the original script was the world (that had been dumbed
down and rendered into pre-fab food) and the inciting incident. But, I did get
paid...

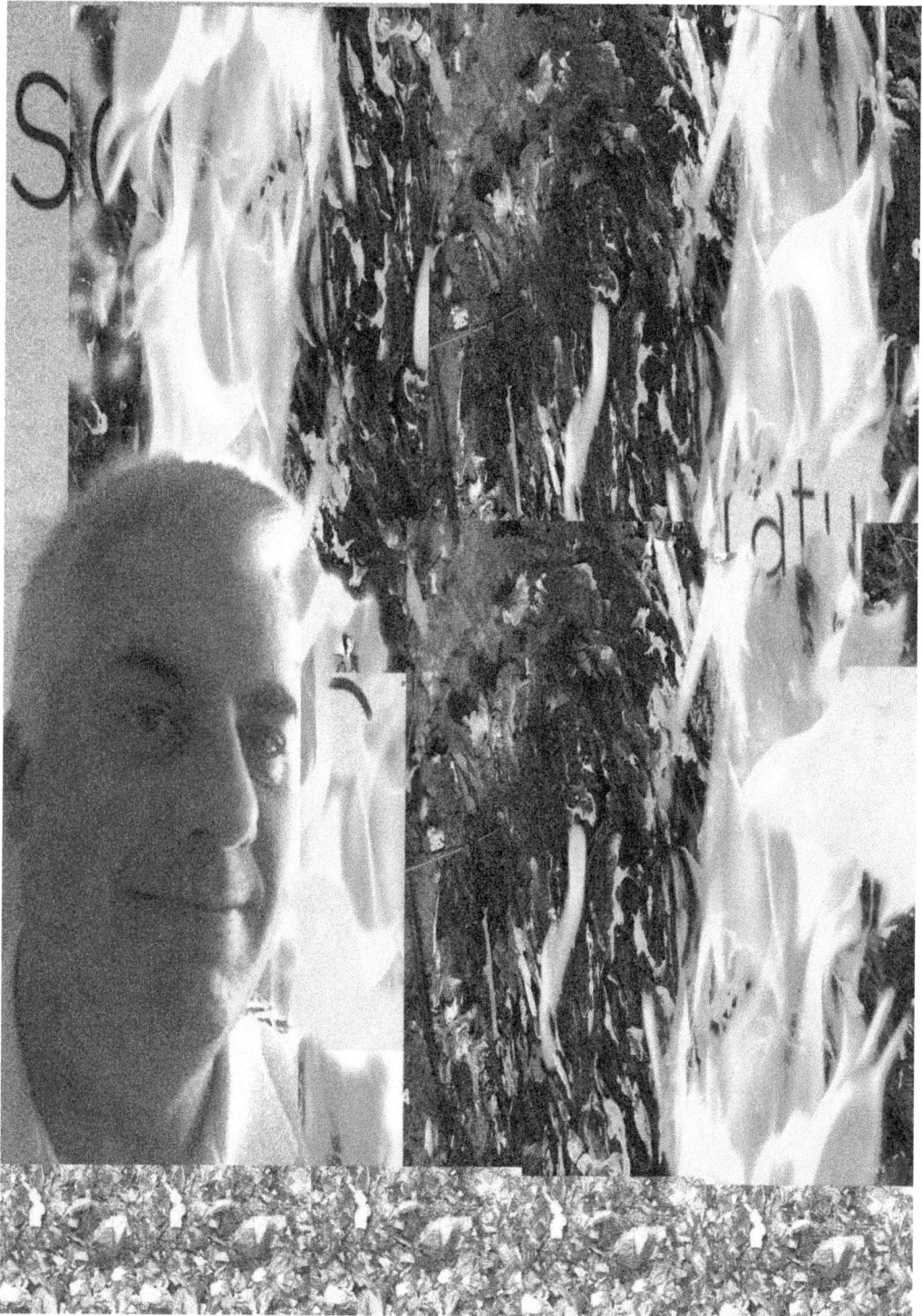

CODA

A list of SWILL volumes:

Original SWILL	issues 1 through 7
SWILL 2011	issues 8 through 12
SWILL 2012	issues 13 through 17
SWILL 2013	issues 18 through 22
SWILL 2014	issues 23 through 26
SWILL 2015	issues 27 through 30
SWILL 2016/2017	issues 31 through 35
SWILL Annuals: Volume 1	issues 36 through 40

Vile Fen Press

a division of Klatha Entertainment an Uldune Media company